The Conversation Series

Copyediting by Matthias Schroers, Matthew Gaskins
Designed at M/M (Paris)
Typesetting by Vera Selitsch

Production by Printmanagement Plitt, Oberhausen

Published by
Verlag der Buchhandlung Walther König, Köln
Ehrenstr. 4, 50672 Cologne, Germany
Tel.: +49 221 20 59 6-53
E-mail: verlag@buchhandlung-walther-koenig.de

The Deutsche Nationalbibliothek lists this publication
in the Deutsche Nationalbibliografie; detailed bibliographic
data are available in the Internet at http://dnb.d-nb.de.

Printed in Germany

Outside Europe
D.A.P./Distributed Art Publishers, Inc., New York
155 Sixth Avenue, New York, NY 10013, USA
Tel.: +1 212 627-1999; Fax: +1 212 627-9484
www.artbook.com

ISBN 978-3-86560-498-9

Gustav Metzger
Hans Ulrich Obrist

16

— The Conversation Series

Verlag der Buchhandlung Walther König, Köln

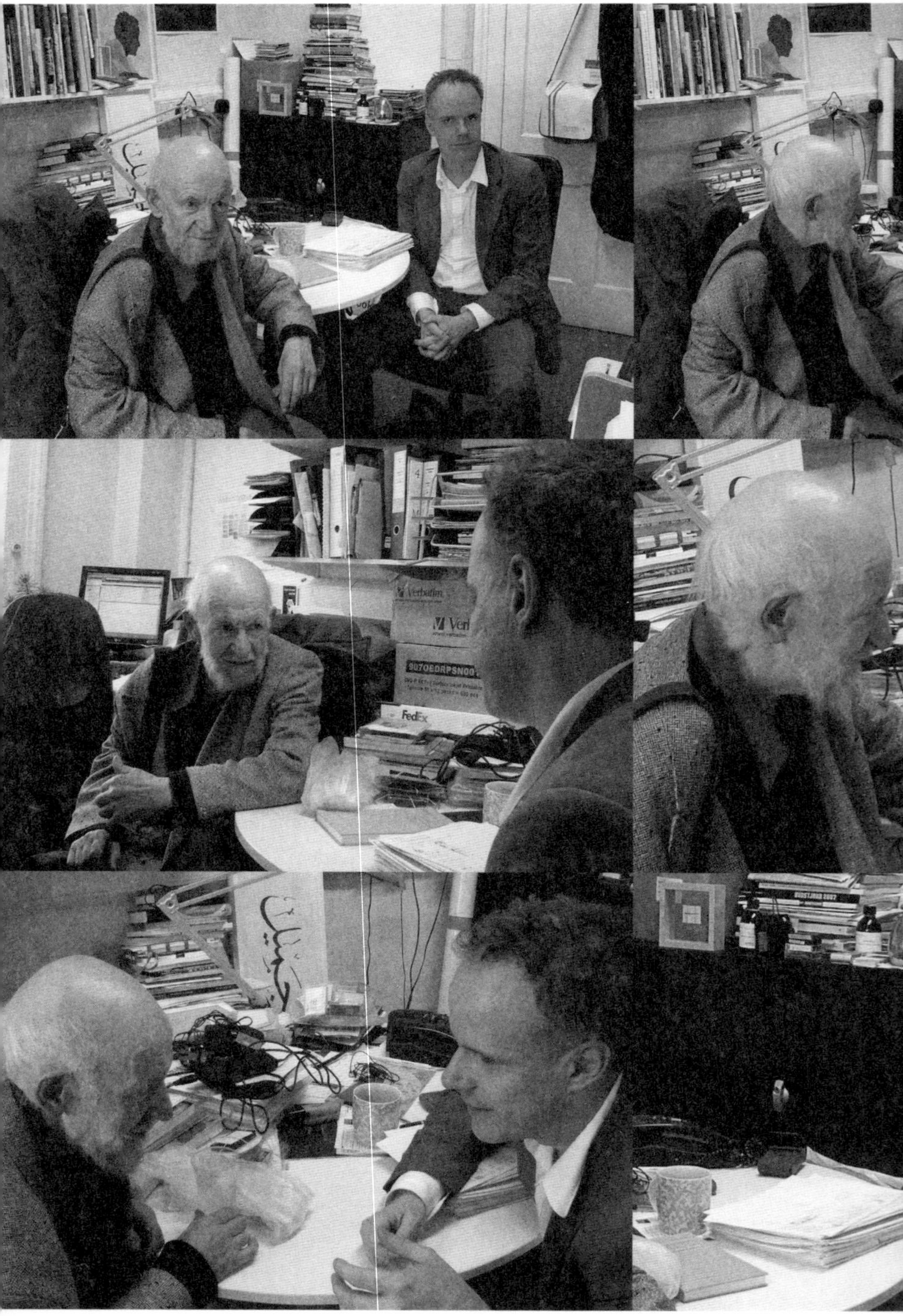
Verbatim
FedEx

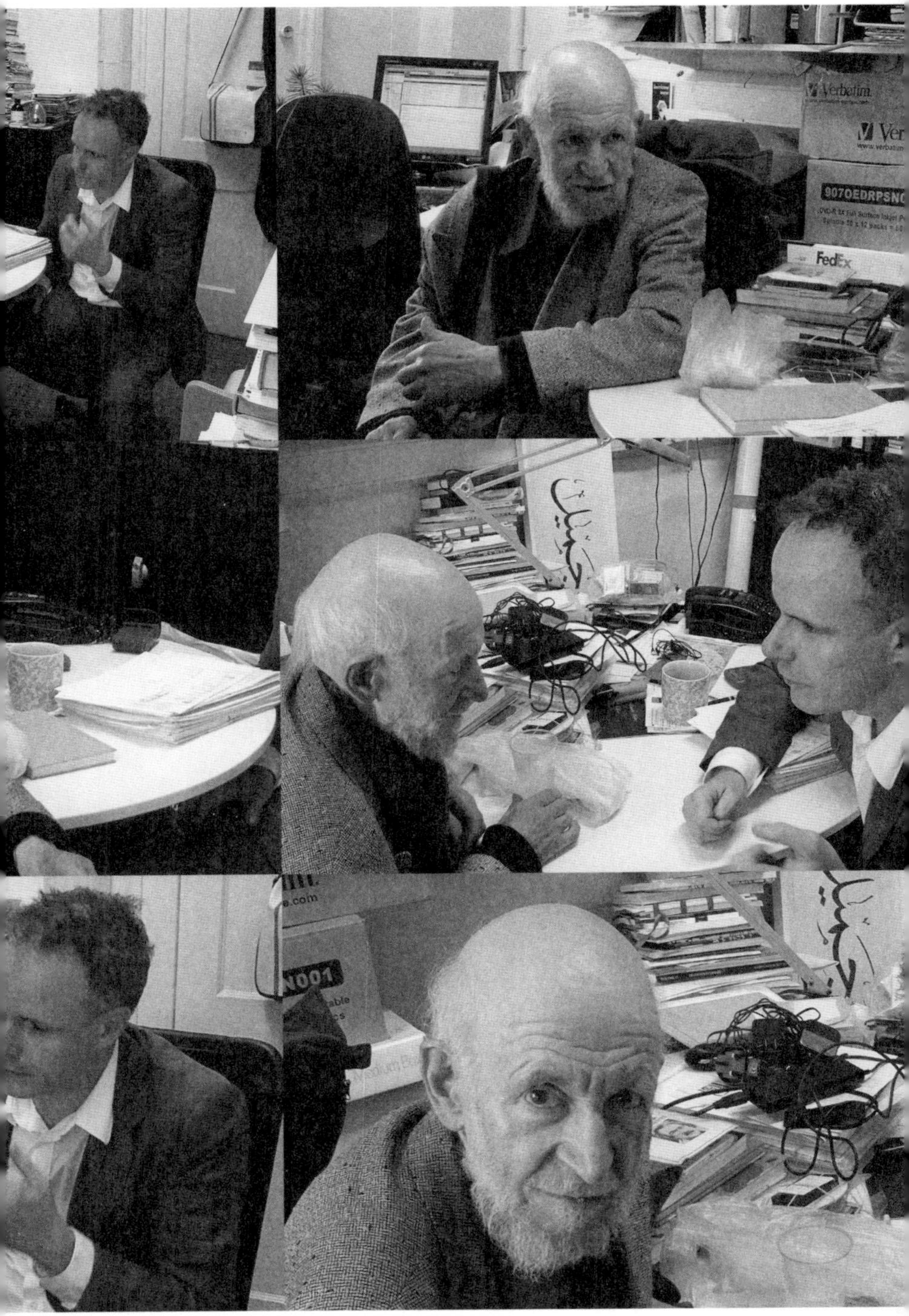
Verbatim
FedEx

The inclusion in this book of advertisements that have appeared in the British national press in recent years relate to my ongoing criticism of capitalist systems. The advertisements include misleading information, and their purpose is to generate maximum profit for the airlines.

Gustav Metzger, London
July 10, 2008

I — Cosmo
Café Cosmo, London, 1996

Hans Ulrich Obrist — **We're conducting this interview in Café Cosmo at Waterloo Station. Could you tell me about the history of Café Cosmo in Hampstead?**

Gustav Metzger — Well, it's very famous. Thousands of people went there during the war, and certainly afterwards, too. People who spoke German met there. In Hampstead you had the cultural centre, which was inspired by the free German communists; the organisation was called the Free German League of Culture.[1] John Heartfield was a leading figure and designed some of their publications. You had liberal Germans, and you probably had right-wing Germans, too—all in

(1) *Exil in Großbritannien. Zur Emigration aus dem nationalsozialistischen Deutschland*, ed. by Gerhard Hirschfeld (Stuttgart: Klett-Cotta, 1983). Engl.: *Exiles in Great Britain. Refugees from Hitler's Germany*, ed. by Gerhard Hirschfeld (Leamington Spa: Berg Publishers et al. 1984).

and out of Hampstead, and in and out of that café. So it's a historic spot that's worth remembering.

Hans Ulrich Obrist — **Can we talk about your unrealised projects?**

Gustav Metzger — The projects are mostly related to auto-destructive art, and none of them have been realised. In fact, none of them have been considered by anyone except me. But what's behind them is the desire to materialise an idea, and an ideal, of auto-destructive art. They're all just words on paper, and words that I've spoken in lectures or private discussions. There are also other unrealised projects that have nothing to do with auto-destructive art, like the floating piece of metal in front of the National Film Theatre, or the liquid crystal projections on the side of the Royal Festival Hall.

Hans Ulrich Obrist — **Please tell me more.**

Gustav Metzger — This is a project from 1970 or 1971. Actually, I went to the Greater London Council, the governing body of London, which was situated in the County Hall, just up the road on the South Bank. I told them I wanted to do certain projects, but they replied, 'You can't.' That was the answer. There were three projects. I told them the project that involved floating metal on the river would look something like this: a piece of iron or steel. 'We don't mind if you do that,' they said, 'but why don't you get an agreement from Trinity House?' So I went as far as seeing Trinity House, and to my surprise they gave me permission. Then I was advised to contact Alistair McAlpine. His firm was building the National Theatre nearby, and he, as you may know, was a great patron of the arts at the time.

Hans Ulrich Obrist — **Would you say that the auto-destructive concept as a whole is an unrealised project?**

Gustav Metzger — Yes, so far. The only realised works were the *Acid Nylon Paintings* [South Bank Demonstration, London, 1961]. These are realisations of auto-destructive art, but they're not perfect realisations. The perfect realisations are monuments. You have to remember, the *Acid Nylon Paintings* were made by hand, but the essence of auto-destructive art is that the hand doesn't play a part in it, except in the construction of the original sculpture. Then it's all automatic. You leave it. The artist no longer touches the work.

Hans Ulrich Obrist — **You've always been reluctant to use the word utopia.**

Gustav Metzger — It's true that I've used the term utopia only very rarely. I've kept shy of it. In fact, it's a word I find rather disturbing; it's so laden with all kinds of past movements. To me it seems unusable. Nevertheless, these projects are utopian in the sense that I've been concerned with the realisation of something in the future—and the future has never happened, and may never happen. So they're utopian in that sense, or in the technical sense, if you like. Certainly you can call it visionary. These are visions, visions of vast monuments, as I describe them—Pharaonic monuments to man's capacity to destroy.[2]

(2) Gustav Metzger, untitled, *Art & Artists* (special issue on DIAS) (London, August 1966).

Hans Ulrich Obrist — **In your writings, you define the concept of auto-destructive art as a very complex theory, as a whole thinking process. Are there different stages in the realisation of these monuments? Perhaps we can discuss the aspect of time.**

Gustav Metzger — Well, it hasn't been realised, but time is at the very centre of the idea. Time, and a way of demonstrating it: demonstrating time, showing time, getting people involved with time. In that sense, it relates to music and to dance, which are art forms I've been very involved in—not as a performer, of course, but as a spectator and listener.

Hans Ulrich Obrist — **But what about changes in time—the change from one moment to another? After all, your monuments are not static sculptures, but are in a state of continual transformation.**

Gustav Metzger — Definitely. The transformation of material is at the very centre of this—material changing its form, shape, and meaning. You respond to each changing form, and to the interaction between changing forms, in a particular manner. At least you can respond if you are sensitive enough, if you are concerned enough. Because of time—either depending on days or weeks or years—there is the opportunity to react differently to the various transformative effects. This is at the centre of my concerns. That's what I meant by the enlargement of the scope of art. And that includes time. Time is involved in everything.

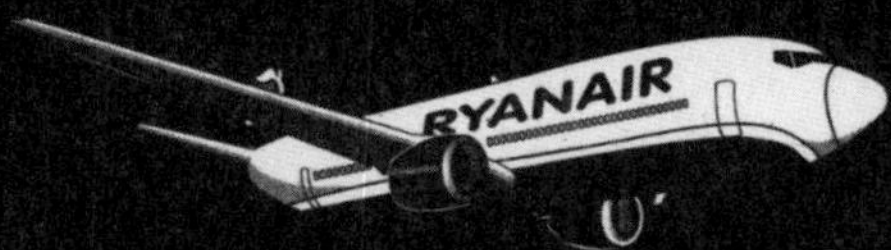

SUMMER

SALE

ONE WAY FROM

£5

TAXES & CHARGES INCL.

RYANAIR

Book until midnight 29.05.08. Subject to availability, terms and conditions.
See Ryanair.com for more details. Flights direct from London (Stansted).

Hans Ulrich Obrist — **Would it be fair to say that you make time monuments rather than space monuments?**

Gustav Metzger — Yes, that's the point. That's the beauty of it—the fact that so many factors are integrated. It's also why I describe auto-destructive art as an extension of capacities. The problem is that people haven't understood this yet. They haven't gone deep enough into the potential that's opened up by auto-destructive art. That's why it's still not there.

Hans Ulrich Obrist — **This is a bit like unbuilt architecture—paper architecture. There's a lot of potential there.**

Gustav Metzger — Yes, but it's bigger than that, because unbuilt architecture is architecture. But here we have something unbuilt that has never existed—that would never exist unless it were made along the lines I've proposed. It's a kind of tragedy. It's a term I use sometimes.

Hans Ulrich Obrist — **As György Kepes has said, it's about going 'beyond the fear of pooling knowledge'.**

Gustav Metzger — I agree that the opportunity for understanding the work is greater now than ever before, but there's still an enormous gap, which can be traced largely to people's resistance to the political views I've expressed over the years. They're pretty extreme, and they're disruptive of the way things are. Most people don't want to know about them, which is one major reason why my work has not been accepted. If I hadn't been in the political arena, I'd probably have been quite successful by now. Here, we can cite the example of

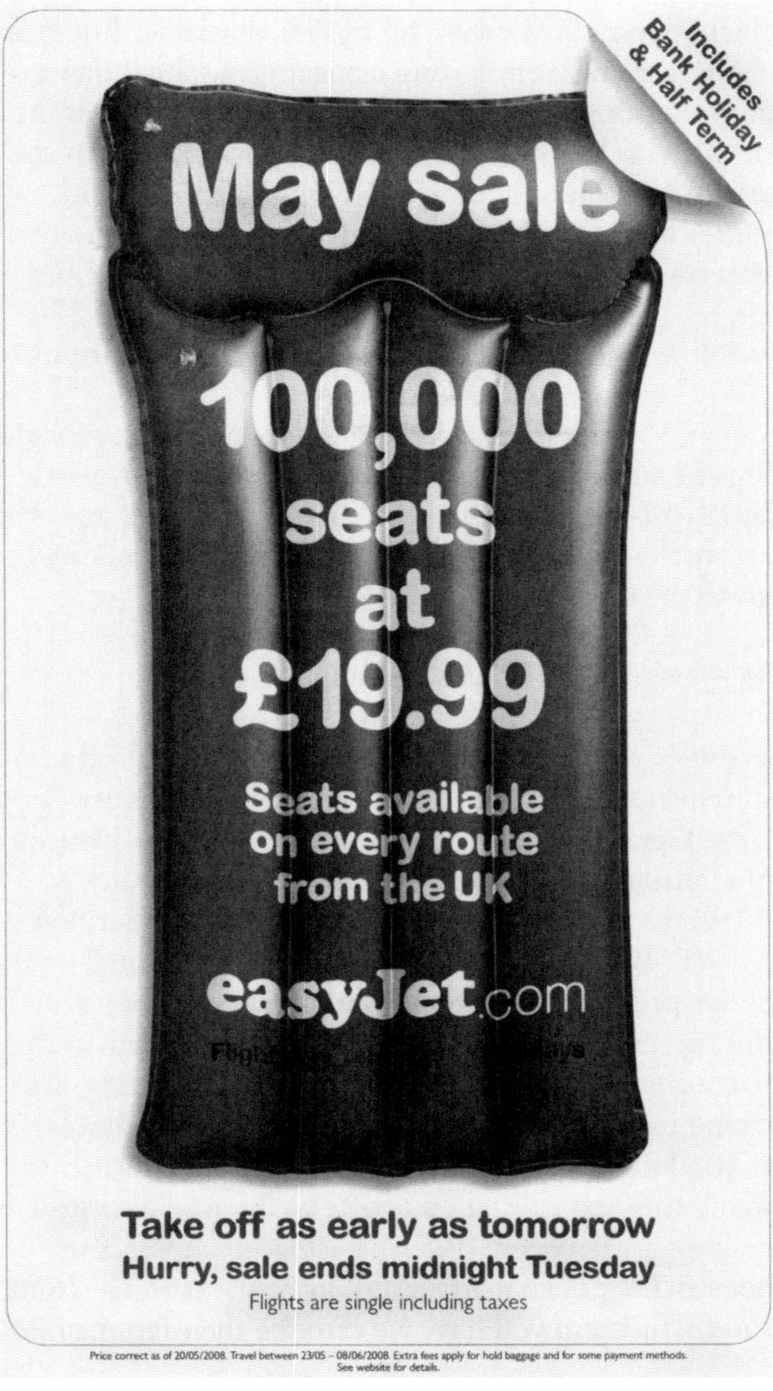
Includes Bank Holiday & Half Term
May sale
100,000 seats at £19.99
Seats available on every route from the UK
easyJet.com
Take off as early as tomorrow
Hurry, sale ends midnight Tuesday
Flights are single including taxes
Price correct as of 20/05/2008. Travel between 23/05 – 08/06/2008. Extra fees apply for hold baggage and for some payment methods. See website for details.

[Jean] Tinguely. I mean, he was an anarchist. But even though he had very strong critical views, he didn't go about writing manifestos or giving lectures. He went on with his work. In contrast, I've always stuck to this attack on society, and people don't like it. I would rather keep to my ideas and give up art than the other way round.

Hans Ulrich Obrist — **That leads to the question about your art strike.**

Gustav Metzger — The art strike was the culmination of feelings I had about not wanting to go into the art world. In 1974 I was at that point of being integrated into the art world, in the sense that in 1972 I had been asked to go to the documenta.

Hans Ulrich Obrist — **By Harald Szeemann?**

Gustav Metzger — Yes. He invited me personally. And there were other exhibitions. In '74 there was this very large German project in London at the ICA [Institute of Contemporary Art] and the Goethe Institute ['Art into Society – Society into Art. Seven German Artists', ICA, London, 1974]. There I was asked—put under pressure, in fact—to participate. There were the two curators, Norman Rosenthal and Christos Joachimides, who had discussions with me for hours, trying to persuade me. Eventually I caved in, but, as you know, I decided not to exhibit, as a gesture. I wrote this text calling on artists of the world to stop making art between 1977 and 1980: three years of not working as an artist [*Years without Art 1977–1980*, 1974]. So there you have an extreme manifestation of my rejection of the way things are, and my attempt to go towards some other ideas.

Hans Ulrich Obrist — **I'd like to return to this notion of auto-destructive art. How would you define it in relation to the pervasiveness of capitalism? Does auto-destructive art aim to abolish the capitalist system?**

Gustav Metzger — That's the central idea, but there are different definitions of this system at different times. There was corporatism, and then you had terms like the global economy, which is still with us. In principle, however, they refer to the same problem: capitalism. The market economy—very popular term at the end of the seventies, early eighties. There's always this attempt not to use the term capitalism.

Hans Ulrich Obrist — **In the sense of a euphemism or evasion?**

Gustav Metzger — Exactly. Of course, capitalism changes. Today it's a system that has triumphed globally. Global economy is the current term. But the problem, which is capitalism, is still there. We have to be opposed to all these terms and to all these developments. It's just one thing: power and domination. The trouble is that there aren't enough people in the art world who think like this.

Hans Ulrich Obrist — **You once mentioned having had conversations with [Joseph] Beuys.**

Gustav Metzger — It was in '72, when he came to the Tate ['Joseph Beuys, 7 Exhibitions', Tate Gallery, London,

1972], and in '74, when he was in London for the German Month at the ICA.

Hans Ulrich Obrist — **Did you basically agree with him?**

Gustav Metzger — We had an important confrontation when we first met in 1972. You've got a picture here in this book of us talking.[3] It was a genuine confrontation. We had never met before, and he knew me by name, but obviously not by sight. Otherwise he would have recognised me. We talked for at least an hour; we were confronting each other. As the text, based on a tape, shows, there were a lot of disagreements between us, and I would suggest that I was considerably more sophisticated in understanding.[4]

Hans Ulrich Obrist — **What was the main disagreement?**

Gustav Metzger — Our main disagreement was about development. I suggested that we shouldn't encourage the so-called Third World to develop along our lines, and here he tended to disagree. He said, and this is a quote, 'If we have goods, we should give them to the poor people so that everyone will benefit'—which means that he never understood the dilemma facing the West. In other words, he didn't understand the crisis which is now so blatant that every schoolchild is aware of it. It's evident from the tape in the Tate Gallery Archive.

(3) Sabine Breitwieser (ed.), *Gustav Metzger. Geschichte Geschichte*, exh. cat. Generali Foundation, Vienna (Ostfildern-Ruit: Hatje Cantz, 2005).
(4) Joseph Beuys, *Information Action, Transcription of the video of Beuys' Action Piece on February 25th 1972 at the Tate Gallery*, Tate Gallery Archive TAV 616AB.

Hans Ulrich Obrist — **Were there other basic disagreements? Were any ecological concerns voiced in the discussion? What about the Green Party?**

Gustav Metzger — Well, we discussed ecological problems, but he didn't understand certain aspects of the crisis at the time. I'm sure he learned as time went on, educating himself and becoming more responsible.

Hans Ulrich Obrist — **Were there other artists with whom you had a dialogue at the time?**

Gustav Metzger — Yes, of course. There was John Latham. I had known him since the early sixties, certainly since '64. As you know, he developed his concept of Artist Placement. My problem with him was that I felt he was too close to the big powers; he was prepared to collaborate closely. We had a public dispute.

Hans Ulrich Obrist — **You disagreed with his concept of infiltrating existing structures.**

Gustav Metzger — I disagreed with the manner of infiltration, the principle of infiltration. However, the article I wrote in response to a major exhibition they had at the Hayward Gallery in the early seventies makes our differences very clear ['Artist Placement Group', *Art&Economics*, Hayward Gallery, London, 1971].[5] My position, and the position I took in the discussion with John Latham, was that if you're going to do the work you're planning to do, then you should go to the company and say, 'We're opposed to you! Yes, that's our

(5) Gustav Metzger, *A critical look at the Artist Placement Group* (London: Studio International, no. 940, January 1972).

position. But we're offering to collaborate on specific projects, which could be interesting for us and possibly helpful to the situation in the world.' He never accepted the challenge I put to him, which is perhaps one reason why we never really worked together.

Hans Ulrich Obrist — **Why did you distance yourself from the Artist Placement Group?**

Gustav Metzger — We did have connections, and we were trying to do things together, but they never materialised. I sort of dropped out. I wasn't the only one; there were others who dropped out of this orbit, too. Of course, I'm not putting down all of their work. Some of it was constructive, and I like John's own work very much. I like his paintings. I'm also very interested in the destructive works he did. I was present at a number of them—a kind of participant, in a sense. I take him very seriously.

Hans Ulrich Obrist — **Didn't the two of you share this anti-Greenberg [Clement Greenberg] bent?**

Gustav Metzger — Well, I wasn't part of that. I mean, I wasn't invited to the Greenberg chew.[6] But I don't have an anti-Greenberg position.

Hans Ulrich Obrist — **You don't?**

Gustav Metzger — I've never taken any position towards critics, of any kind, because I don't think it's my job.

(6) In 1966 John Latham and a group of students dismembered and chewed up a library copy of Clement Greenberg's *Art and Culture*. The resulting artwork, *Still and Chew. Art and Culture 1966–1967*, is now in the collection of the Museum of Modern Art in New York.

Maybe I haven't got the capacity to do so. I'm not like some of the American artists who are polemical in the art field. I'm much more concerned with the outside world than with the inner world of art. So it's not my job to attack either artists or critics. I have attacked institutions, however, but that's something else. I also have to admit that I've hardly read any Greenberg, even to this day.

Hans Ulrich Obrist — **But in the beginning you were working with David Bomberg and you said you wanted to become a sculptor. So how did this first major destructive drive enter into your work? Did it come out of a disagreement with Bomberg? I'd be very interested in knowing more about the origins of your auto-destructive project.**

Gustav Metzger — The origins are very clear. It was a vision I had in the late summer of 1959, when I returned to London. For many years I had lived in King's Lynn, a small market town in East Anglia, but in early 1959 I left. I was living in a beautiful big house there, with a studio and workshops and so on, but I gave it all up. I was very poor and isolated, but I still had a very good time in 1959. I won't go into the whole story, but it's connected with a small artist café called 14 Monmouth Street, where I exhibited some paintings I had done in King's Lynn ['Three Paintings by G. Metzger', 1959]. Then I exhibited the cardboards ['Cardboards exhibition', 1959], which are illustrated here. I met two young people in the café who were kind of neo-Dadaists. They weren't fully professional. They showed junk sculptures. One day we were sitting around, and after they had shown their work and

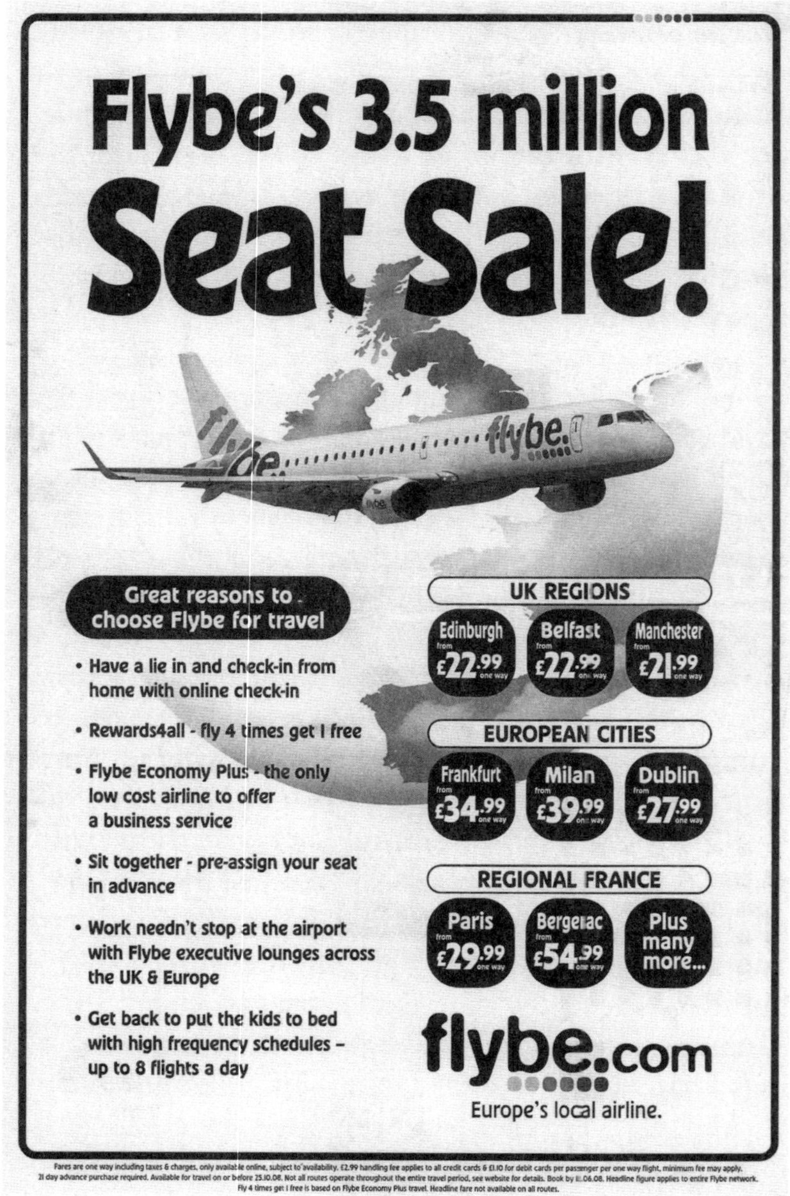
Flybe's 3.5 million
Seat Sale!
flybe.
flybe.
Great reasons to choose Flybe for travel
• Have a lie in and check-in from home with online check-in
• Rewards4all - fly 4 times get 1 free
• Flybe Economy Plus - the only low cost airline to offer a business service
• Sit together - pre-assign your seat in advance
• Work needn't stop at the airport with Flybe executive lounges across the UK & Europe
• Get back to put the kids to bed with high frequency schedules – up to 8 flights a day
UK REGIONS
Edinburgh from £22.99 one way
Belfast from £22.99 one way
Manchester from £21.99 one way
EUROPEAN CITIES
Frankfurt from £34.99 one way
Milan from £39.99 one way
Dublin from £27.99 one way
REGIONAL FRANCE
Paris from £29.99 one way
Bergerac from £54.99 one way
Plus many more...
flybe.com
Europe's local airline.
Fares are one way including taxes & charges, only available online, subject to availability. £2.99 handling fee applies to all credit cards & £1.10 for debit cards per passenger per one way flight, minimum fee may apply.
21 day advance purchase required. Available for travel on or before 25.10.08. Not all routes operate throughout the entire travel period, see website for details. Book by 11.06.08. Headline figure applies to entire Flybe network.
Fly 4 times get 1 free is based on Flybe Economy Plus travel. Headline fare not available on all routes.

I had shown some of mine, one of them said, 'I think we should make an exhibition of paintings, and once it opens we'll burn them.' That was a kind of spark for me. It wasn't the first time I had thought of destruction, but it was this specific idea. Within a month or two, I had the idea of creating a sculpture that would disintegrate over the course of the exhibition. So I would make a sculpture, not much bigger than this—maybe twice the height—for the London Group, which has annual or biannual exhibitions. The idea was to have some kind of built-in chemical or mechanical system that would allow you to see the transformation after two or three weeks. This was actually the origin of auto-destructive art—not an idea, but a work, a sculpture. And based on the idea of that sculpture, I began to develop a theory, the first manifesto, which was published to coincide with the private view of the 'Cardboard exhibition' at 14 Monmouth Street on 9 November, 1959. It was one sheet of typed paper with two texts.[7] From that point onwards, I didn't stop thinking about the idea of auto-destructive art. You asked me earlier about the first acid painting. I painted the first one in 1960, about seven months after the first manifesto. Now that's closer to Bomberg. When you look at photographs of that first painting, you might think that I was painting in his style.

Hans Ulrich Obrist — **You wrote about Bomberg in the early fifties. What interested you about him?**

Gustav Metzger — First of all, he was my teacher. I had many teachers, but he was the main one—and the one I

(7) Gustav Metzger, *Cardboards selected and arranged by G. Metzger – Auto-Destructive Art* (London, 1959).

was interested in more than any other. He always influenced the way I was painting or drawing. He was also a friend and a supporter. He arranged for me to get a grant for three years. He worked with me, but also for me. And he became a kind of father figure. There was a difference in age, but he was of Polish-Jewish origin, just like my family. There was so much that brought us together. At the same time, we had quite a few disagreements. I left his class on several occasions.

Hans Ulrich Obrist — **What were the reasons for these disagreements?**

Gustav Metzger — Well, if you're a young man—and I met him when I was nineteen—you inevitably rebel against the older person.

Hans Ulrich Obrist — **Just as a son rebels against his father?**

Gustav Metzger — Exactly. You rebel against the father, and you rebel against the teacher. That was part of it. In the end, though, in the early fifties there were three years when he had two evening classes a week at the Borough Polytechnic. I attended all of them, even though I didn't live in London. Sometimes I travelled fifty miles to get to his class. So as you can see, I was fully committed and reconciled to the relationship of teacher and student. But then things got very complicated.

Hans Ulrich Obrist — **In what way?**

Gustav Metzger — The final disagreement was... Originally, in 1948, Bomberg had a group that the students called the Borough Group. We formed the Borough Bottega in 1953, and I was the driving force behind it. I was also behind the idea that we students should do something together to recognise Bomberg. So we established this Borough Bottega in the summer. It was a long summer, and it took us a dozen meetings to go through the idea and to establish a constitution and arrange an exhibition, which was held in October and November of 1953 ['Borough Bottega', Berkeley Galleries, London, 1953]. But after all that, I came to the conclusion that there was a fundamental problem with the entire situation. Bomberg wanted too special a place for himself and his family, which wasn't right. We had decided—I had decided—that the Borough Bottega would try to put him on the map, but as the meetings proceeded, and as we formed the constitution, I realised that he, in an extraordinary, egoistical manner, was trying to dominate the group to an extent that I could no longer accept. So I resigned, though even then I said, 'Look, I'm resigning from the group, but that doesn't mean I don't want to continue supporting you.' I'd left London for a number of reasons and had moved to King's Lynn. Then I got a letter from Bomberg saying that he could no longer have any contact with me. I can't quote it now, but it's something like 'You've taken up too much of my life. Goodbye.' So he ended the relationship. I had changed my relationship to the group, but I hadn't cut any ties. My correspondence with Bomberg is in the Tate Gallery Archive. It's all documented.

Hans Ulrich Obrist — We often discussed painting and politics—the whole notion of political art. Can paintings or sculptures still carry a political message? Can they still trigger a state crisis like the one sparked by [Théodore] Géricault's *The Raft of the Medusa* in the nineteenth century?

Gustav Metzger — This is precisely why I moved away from painting—from Bomberg, if you like—towards auto-destructive art. This is the crisis I've lived through. All those years of my being a student, starting in January 1945, I asked myself how art can contribute to saving society, to changing society. This is what I asked myself every day, more or less, all those years. And auto-destructive art was the liberating ideal for me. The tragedy is that society didn't recognise this potential. Or to put it another way, society is clever enough to see the potential and stop it, because that's how it operates: society is a self-protecting organism. As soon as it, in a broad sense, wants you to stop, they kill or imprison you—they send you to a mad house or make you ill, or they ignore you. Nobody killed or imprisoned me, although they could have done so, but they certainly ignored me. I'm not blaming everything on the outside, though, because I have my own failures. As I told you, I didn't send works to Pontus Hultén when he asked me. I didn't take advantage of other opportunities. So there's a self-destructive trend in me, too, inside my own person. I accept that and have to live with it.

Hans Ulrich Obrist — You then initiated a legendary symposium based on destruction in art. Otto Muehl told me a lot about it; it was a very important event [DIAS Destruction in Art Symposium, Africa Centre, London, 1966].

Gustav Metzger — Yes, it arose from the realisation that there were so many artists in the world who destroyed things at some point, quite independently of auto-destructive art. The artists were not working with auto-destructive art. That's quite clear. But the vast majority were using elements of destruction, physically damaging their work and opening it up.

Hans Ulrich Obrist — **What about [Lucio] Fontana's influence?**

Gustav Metzger — Fontana, indeed. I talked to Fontana once. Surely there is a destructive element. He repeatedly said to me, 'No, I reject this interpretation completely. It's only a constructive process where I liberate space behind the cut. In and behind the cut there is space which I liberate.' Of course I have to accept this explanation, but Fontana is on the edge of destruction. And there's [Raphael Montañez] Ortiz, who tears furniture. I've seen it in London.

Hans Ulrich Obrist — **What about [Alberto] Burri?**

Gustav Metzger — Burri is certainly close to Fontana. There's a close connection, insofar as they make something that stays, is fixed, and becomes a work of art. And there's John Latham and [Bernard] Aubertin with their book burnings. You can go on and on and on. So the idea in August 1966 was to bring this together into one platform. You can read all about it in Kristine Stiles's dissertation.[8]

Hans Ulrich Obrist — **About the Viennese actionists, too?**

(8) Kristine Stiles, *The Destruction in Art Symposium (DIAS); The Radical Cultural Project of Event-Structured Live Art* (Berkeley: University of California, 1987).

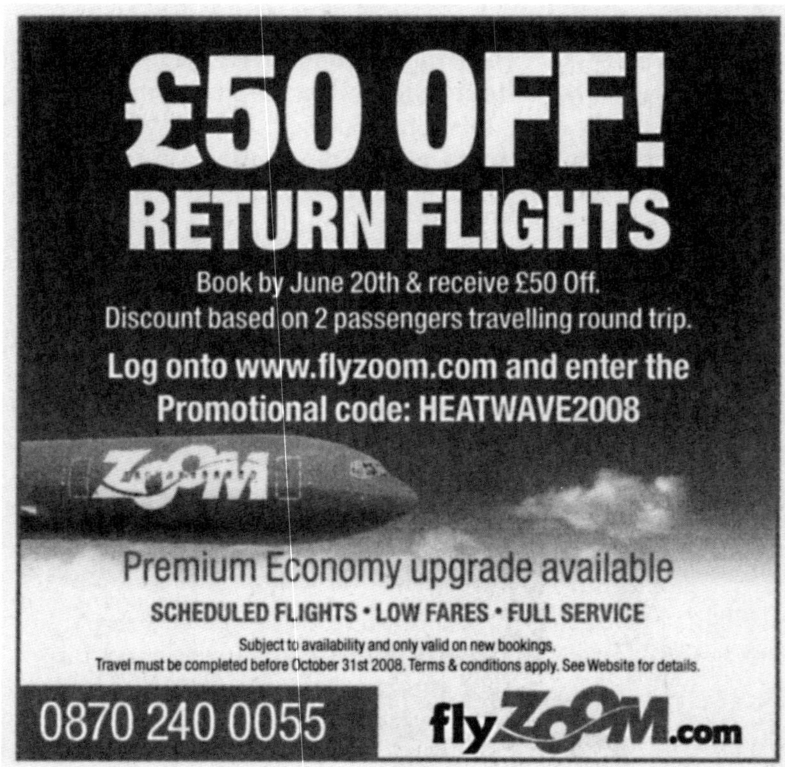
£50 OFF!
RETURN FLIGHTS
Book by June 20th & receive £50 Off.
Discount based on 2 passengers travelling round trip.
Log onto www.flyzoom.com and enter the
Promotional code: HEATWAVE2008
ZOOM
Premium Economy upgrade available
SCHEDULED FLIGHTS • LOW FARES • FULL SERVICE
Subject to availability and only valid on new bookings.
Travel must be completed before October 31st 2008. Terms & conditions apply. See Website for details.
0870 240 0055
flyZOOM.com

Gustav Metzger — Yes. I don't know if you've seen the new book called *The Destruction of Art* by [Dario] Gamboni.[9] Do get it while you are in London. It's certainly in all the big book shops. It's a good book.

Hans Ulrich Obrist — **Your entire oeuvre is about transformation.**

Gustav Metzger — You've got the painting right there that illustrates this best. In this first public painting I did in the summer of 1960, I painted with strokes, with brushes [first *Lecture/Demonstration*, Temple Gallery, London]. One year later, in the open air, I changed my approach and my technique [*South Bank Demonstration*, South Bank, London, 1961]. Instead of one painting, one screen, I had three screens. And I didn't paint, but sprayed. It's a completely different way of working and thinking, and it leads to the total obliteration of the artwork. We're seeing the work in progress, but in the end all you had was some strips left. It was never frozen in time, and it was never meant to be.

Hans Ulrich Obrist — **Are you going to reconstruct, or remake, the 1961 event in Los Angeles?**

Gustav Metzger — Yes, as closely as possible. That's what I have been asked to do. In principle, I've accepted the challenge, with all of the problems it entails. But this is a work that goes way beyond Bomberg, who never conceived of it and perhaps wouldn't have wanted it. In Roy Oxlade's dissertation, there's a section where he refers to my activities at the end of the Borough

(9) Dario Gamboni, *The Destruction of Art. Iconoclasm and Vandalism since the French Revolution* (London: Reaktion, 2007).

Bottega and says, 'This destructiveness of Metzger is a signal that came out later. When Metzger did this auto-destructive art, he revealed his destructivity.'[10] I know that Mrs Bomberg, Bomberg's wife, regarded my new work as unacceptable, and it's possible that Bomberg might have felt the same way. He died in 1957, two years before I became involved in this, so it raises the question of how this relates to my teaching. But it is a rejection of my studies; I had to go beyond them. This is the point: young artists have to go beyond their masters. It's a statement that Bomberg made repeatedly and in different ways.

Hans Ulrich Obrist — **Your works are not an accumulation of static objects, but the result of much more active processes. This also leads to the second distinction between your work and that of many participants in the Destruction in Art Symposium. In fact, some artists in the sixties and seventies did performances that were very artistic and auto-destructive, but they were performances in themselves—they didn't invite the viewer to participate. Since the sixties, and maybe even since the fifties, your work has always been firmly rooted in the realm of participation. Could you tell me more about this aspect?**

Gustav Metzger — The idea at the centre of these auto-destructive monuments is to provide people with another vision, to offer them something they haven't already got—something significant on the aesthetic level, but also on the political plane. This is already a plus. If you see something novel, well, it must be good, I suggest. They see something challenging, so it challenges their perception of daily reality, which is

(10) Roy Oxlade, *Bomberg's Papers – The Spirit in the Mass (A Commentary Together with Transcriptions of Various Previously Unpublished Notes)*, PhD Thesis (Royal College of Art, London, 1980).

good. It offers them a visual experience they can't get anywhere else. All this is free, because we're dealing with public sculpture.

Hans Ulrich Obrist — **This notion of participation is also very strong in your current work, *Historic Photographs.* There you have images to walk into, to crawl into, just as you showed them in 'Life/Live' in Paris ['Life/Live. La scène artistique au Royaume-Uni en 1996', Musée d'Art moderne de la Ville de Paris, 1996].**

Gustav Metzger — To respond, to interact—yes, auto-destructive art is concerned with giving to people, getting them absorbed in something unusual, and, of course, changing their political views. The last point applies to my present work, doesn't it? In Paris I confronted present-day Israel and Nazi Austria of the past in the show that Laurence Bossé and you co-curated. Of course, some people understand the connections and others don't. My challenge is to make people see connections, to see the differences, and to interact and hopefully transform their being through confronting these very difficult works. These are very difficult works, don't you think?

Hans Ulrich Obrist — **Yes, uncomfortable. But there's a paradox, because they're very uncomfortable, and yet the people who did interact did so with great enthusiasm and got very involved. Usually there was never one person alone; there was a process where two or three people went in.**

Gustav Metzger — Yes, but let me say this: a number of people came up and said how much they liked it, how highly they rated my exhibits. I asked some of them if they had gone in, and some said yes. Then I asked, 'Did you crawl in?' But nobody I talked to actually admitted that. There was one person, for example, who rated the *Historic Photographs* very highly, and I asked him, 'Did you crawl in?' He looked at me aghast and said, 'There are three things I never do, and one of them is to crawl.' He was an Englishman—middle class, respectable, somebody high up in the art world. I can understand him, but it shows you…

Hans Ulrich Obrist — **Is it about guilt in public space?**

Gustav Metzger — Yes, but it has to do with Willy Brandt kneeling down in Warsaw—very public, as head of the German government. He knelt down in front of this monument. It's world famous. I think what I'm doing is offering everybody the chance to kneel down in front of history. Just walking in means accepting the heaviness, the weight of history—which is a good thing for people to do, to go in and confront the past. Presenting oneself against that history means that you have a chance to transform yourself. You have a chance to change. This is really what my work is about: offering people the chance to change through a work of art. In that sense, I'm fulfilling a responsibility I took upon myself when I first became an artist. What can I do as an artist to help society? Can I help prevent future wars? Can art do it instead of just politics? And I said to myself, 'Art can do it. Art must do it. And I must be one of the artists who do it.'

Hans Ulrich Obrist — **It's about art changing the world.**

Gustav Metzger — It's about art changing the world and me as an individual artist facing up to the challenge. I believe that, through auto-destructive art, I've succeeded at least in formulating an idea and an ideal through which this can come about. In that sense, I'm reasonably content—looking back, and also looking forward to my future works—that I'm on the right track.

Hans Ulrich Obrist — **Does this mean that auto-destructive art is only just beginning?**

Gustav Metzger — Yes, in a sense. And with your book, hopefully, somebody who is out there, listening, waiting, may respond to this cry of mine.[11] It's always possible.

Hans Ulrich Obrist — **So it boils down to triggering a process.**

Gustav Metzger — Yes.

Hans Ulrich Obrist — **The Paris piece, but also other pieces, trigger reactions between the spaces so that people engage in dialogue.**

Gustav Metzger — That's what I'm working on. My job is to draw people in so that they can interact and work towards social change. That's a principle I'm committed to. It doesn't mean I won't ever do paintings, because I believe—I've always believed—that painting and sculpture make a major contribution. In all my talks to students, all these decades, I've never said anything else. So one day I'm quite prepared to go into some room and see if I can paint. If the paintings

(11) Hans Ulrich Obrist, Guy Tortosa (eds.), *Unbuilt Roads. 107 Unrealized Projects* (Ostfildern-Ruit: Hatje Cantz, 1997).

aren't good, I don't have to exhibit them. If they are, I will. I don't see any contradiction. Any form of art has validity, and I'm open to change in the future.

Hans Ulrich Obrist — **It seems to be less about being against painting, or against sculpture, but more like a mix of media—something that's in between. How do you see this in connection with Dick Higgins's theory of intermedia, where everything is in between?**

Gustav Metzger — It's perfectly acceptable, and of course I'm in that position now, influenced by newspapers, historical photographs, current events, and the whole history of art or culture. Again, cosmology is part of this. Cosmology goes back for tens of thousands of years; it's concerned with the beginning and ending of time and space and life. It's an area I've reflected on quite a bit over the past few years. A large number of people—not just scientists—are learning about this, reading books, watching television, listening to the radio. This way of understanding the world is very close to auto-destructive art. Now we accept that the world started with nothing and that it will end with nothing, but it's going through enormous transformations that involve destructivity. I see the fact that there's now a world movement concerned with these fundamentals as a powerful confirmation of my position in art. What's so important about this is that people are becoming more honest. Until recently, culture was an attempt to escape from the realisation that we're finite; culture was the idea that we would have these monuments forever.

BIGGEST EVER SEAT SALE!

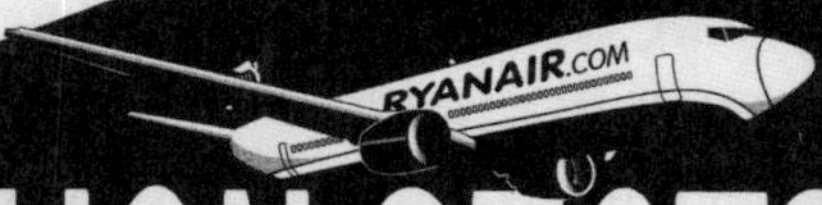

6 MILLION SEATS

JUST PAY TAXES & CHARGES

TRAVEL DATE	AVAILABILITY	TRAVEL DATE	AVAILABILITY
1ST OCT - 7TH OCT	EXCELLENT	8TH DEC - 15TH DEC	EXCELLENT
8TH OCT - 15TH OCT	EXCELLENT	16TH DEC - 23RD DEC	SOME
16TH OCT - 23RD OCT	GOOD	24TH DEC - 31ST DEC	SOME
24TH OCT - 31ST OCT	SOME	1ST JAN - 7TH JAN	SOME
1ST NOV - 7TH NOV	SOME	8TH JAN - 15TH JAN	VERY GOOD
8TH NOV - 15TH NOV	EXCELLENT	16TH JAN - 23RD JAN	EXCELLENT
16TH NOV - 23RD NOV	EXCELLENT	24TH JAN - 31ST JAN	EXCELLENT
24TH NOV - 30TH NOV	EXCELLENT	1ST FEB - 7TH FEB	VERY GOOD
1ST DEC - 7TH DEC	EXCELLENT		

SALE EXTENDED
UNTIL MIDNIGHT THURSDAY!

ALL ROUTES AVAILABLE

TRAVEL OCT '07 - FEB '08

RYANAIR.COM

Book until midnight 13.09.07. Terms & conditions apply. See Ryanair.com for more details. Flights direct from London (Stansted).

Hans Ulrich Obrist — **Like an illusion of infinity?**

Gustav Metzger — Yes, the Renaissance. Every great burst of art has been based on the idea that we have made it—that we have achieved the absolute in books, in philosophy, in art. Isn't that the feeling you get when you look at different major cultures? Today we're thinking that it's all over. It doesn't matter, you see? There was a time a few decades ago when people thought they were all so clever: 'We know the earth will be burnt, but we'll escape.' Now, slowly people are beginning to think, 'Alright, we can do that, and will do that, but wherever we go, we're trapped.' Because, in the end, everything will end in nothing. It might not happen for a hundred million years, but we might as well give up now, because we will never succeed in permanent life. When this idea percolates—and it hasn't percolated yet—people will accept that, and they may begin to think along the lines that I've begun to think: that we might as well abandon all these dreams of permanent life and technology, and just live—live for the present and enjoy ourselves, and not kill ourselves with the ideal of immortality.

Hans Ulrich Obrist — **Hakim Bey talks about 'immediatism'.**

Gustav Metzger — Yes, I'm going to read that book.[12] I liked his lecture enormously. We're in a very fascinating stage in culture where people are finally facing these fundamentals—that we will die as a species. So why not just live for the present? Why not have a good time on earth rather than keep escaping into space,

(12) Hakim Bey, *Immediatism* (New York: Libertarian Book Club, 1992).

into some unknown, endless future? When this is realised, and I think it will take another twenty years, the ideals of living on the land, living close to nature, living in a simplified manner, will start to grow. We're becoming more realistic. We're facing up to the dangers of bio-technology. Thirty years ago we didn't do that. Now everybody is talking about it. This is facing up to reality—facing up in the right way, in a constructive manner. So in that sense I feel history is on my side, and it's one of the reasons I have more confidence than I did twenty years ago. Twenty years ago we had the Cold War; there was so much uncertainty about everything.

II — Extremes Touch / Laboratorium[13]
Oxford, 1999

Hans Ulrich Obrist — **Could you tell me about the genesis of your 1968 laboratory exhibition?**

Gustav Metzger — As you know, there was a major conference—the Dialectics of Liberation—in July 1967 at the Roundhouse in London. It took place at the same time that John Sharkey and I were before the Old Bailey in connection with the Hermann Nitsch event at the Destruction in Art Symposium the year before. I used to go over to the Roundhouse after the hearing, and one afternoon, a young man asked me if I would like to have an exhibition in the course of this art festival at Swansea University, to open in January 1968. The young man was called John Plant, and he

(13) First published in Hans Ulrich Obrist & Barbara Vanderlinden (eds.), *Laboratorium* (Cologne: DuMont, 2001).

arranged the programme. And so I spent several weeks in Swansea preparing an exhibition.

Hans Ulrich Obrist — **You mentioned that when you went to Swansea they showed you a very specific building. Was it a real laboratory?**

Gustav Metzger — I didn't know what kind of exhibition I wanted to do, and John Plant didn't know either. So I went and started looking round the university for a good space. One day I just happened to open a door that revealed a laboratory, a beautiful and pristine laboratory that had never been used—virgin territory. I requested permission to use it and was given the go-ahead.

Hans Ulrich Obrist — **So your exhibition was the first activity in a newly built, virgin laboratory.**

Gustav Metzger — That's right. It was called Filtration Laboratory and was designed specifically to investigate the flow of air and water. It had extraordinary technical facilities. The jets of water could be controlled to a very fine degree; they could be very powerful or incredibly delicate. The same with the air pressure. I used these possibilities to make works that already existed vaguely in my mind, but were produced within the context of these opportunities.

Hans Ulrich Obrist — **Basically, the tools and instruments in this laboratory triggered new works that you probably never would have created otherwise.**

Gustav Metzger — That's correct. I could never have done them, and probably never would have conceived them.

Hans Ulrich Obrist — **Could you describe some of the works? I know the water drop piece, for example.**

Gustav Metzger — The water drop piece started with the commonplace observation that when water is dropped onto a cooker hotplate, it stays there for a moment before it starts running off and dispersing. I thought it would be very beautiful to have a drop—the biggest drop that wouldn't disperse and run off. The laboratory installation made that possible: I could take the water from the overhead pipe, direct it down a thin grey plastic tube towards the hotplate, and by controlling the flow of water, managed to build up a bubble that stayed for quite a time.

Hans Ulrich Obrist — **You made the impermanent permanent?**

Gustav Metzger — It was very beautiful to have this element of stability, which at the same time was rotating like mad—you could see that, from inside, it was explosive. Another main work was a jet of water going from one side to another. Now you wouldn't normally have a jet of water in an exhibition, but I had one in this exhibition space. In relation to the jet, there was a plastic tube hanging down from the ceiling, and the airflow went across the ceiling in another pipe, right along the entire laboratory. I managed to fit that plastic tube into the bigger air pipe, and by putting air into the tube, it began to revolve like a snake around itself, forming a kind of dance. Depending on the volume of air, which I had complete control over just by manipulating a tap, I could make this a very gentle dance, but the more air I put in, the wilder it got. So you had this vertical jet of air hitting, merging with the horizontal jet of water. It was an amazing sight.

Hans Ulrich Obrist — **Were you able to regulate it?**

Gustav Metzger — I could regulate both the water and the air supply.

Hans Ulrich Obrist — **Were these the main components of the piece?**

Gustav Metzger — Yes, but then there was another refinement. The space was very long, and as you came in you were faced by a long row of windows with venetian blinds. The blinds were down, it was winter, and I noticed that at noon the light would come in at a certain angle, creating an extraordinary rainbow effect. It was quite fascinating.

Hans Ulrich Obrist — **That's very interesting because Andreas Slominski and Damien Hirst both talked about rainbows in exhibitions.**

Gustav Metzger — This, of course, relates to people like Turner and other nineteenth-century artists who were obsessed with the rainbow—and to Goethe, as well, who was also working on the subject. The next exhibit was concerned with floating three pieces of polystyrene off the ground. The pieces were rectangular in shape. At each of the four corners of the object, a stream of compressed air hit the ground and formed a cushion of air floating the piece. It remained in place and gave a very restful impression. The beautiful thing about this was that it was positioned in relation to the next work—two of the hotplates. They both appeared stable, yet they were in fact boiling hot, with powerful internal forces, and here were jets of air hitting the ground and lifting up the two sheets of different sizes. So we had three main exhibits. Then there was the cube, a recreation of what you saw in Oxford—a cube of clear plastic with mica pieces rotating through jets of air. Then, at the farthest end, we built a cubicle. I had excellent technical assistance—the technical staff of the university assisted me with the project.

Hans Ulrich Obrist — **In our previous conversation, you spoke about the importance of working with technicians rather than scientists.**

Gustav Metzger — I managed, partly through intuition, to solve the key issues. It wasn't as if the technicians came up and asked, 'Why don't you do this?' They never came up with ideas for individual works. In fact, the chief technician, who was particularly interested and supportive, said the best way to float the plastic would be to lift it up with jets of air from below. I told him I didn't want it like that, but would rather have the air hitting the ground to lift it. He said it would never work. Now I could have asked him to go and work it out for me, but eventually I tested it myself. To his surprise it worked extremely well. In fact, it wouldn't have worked his way, because it would have led to instability—and it would have taken ages to make a system to put the air underneath. In any case,

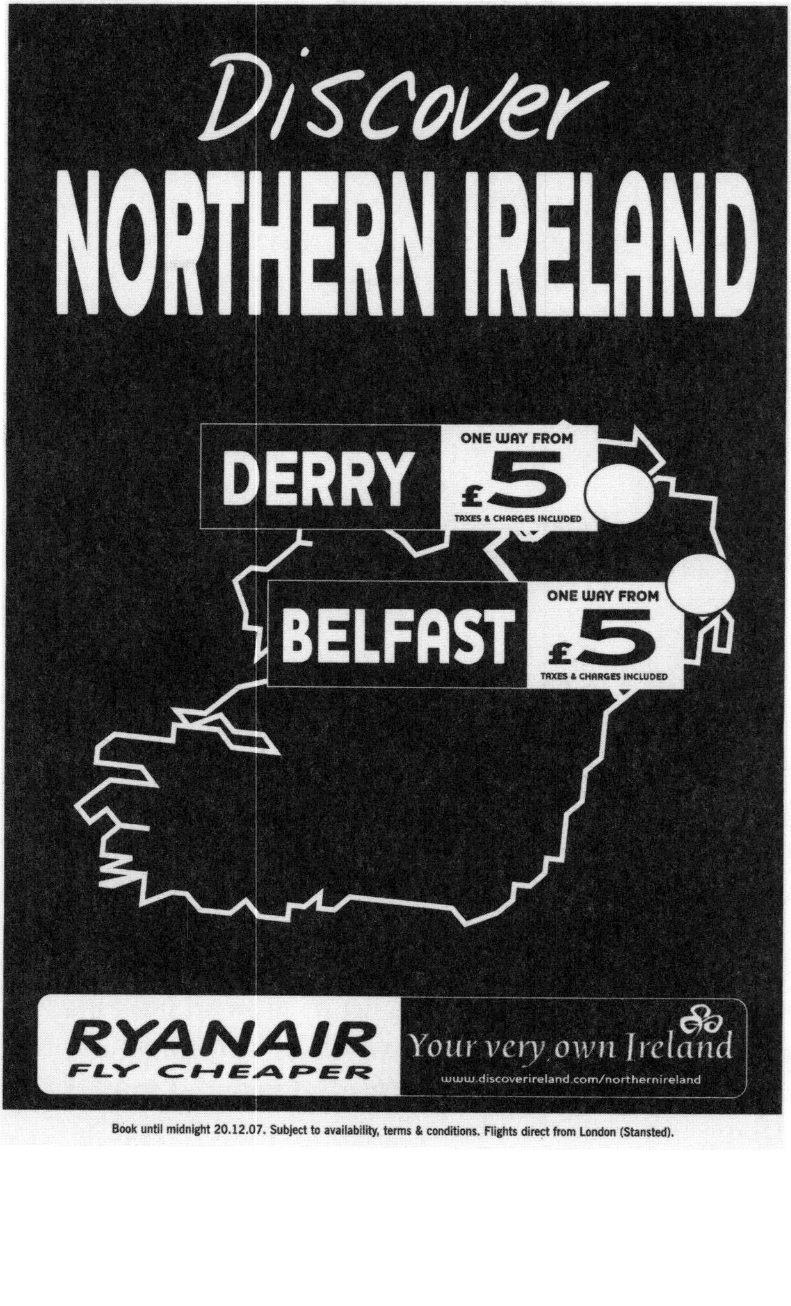

Book until midnight 20.12.07. Subject to availability, terms & conditions. Flights direct from London (Stansted).

2 MILLION SEATS

JUST PAY TAXES & CHARGES

Flights from LONDON (STANSTED)

AARHUS	BILLUND	DUBLIN	GRENOBLE	LA ROCHELLE	OSLO (TORP)	REUS (BARCELONA)	TAMPERE
ALGHERO (SARDINIA)	BOLOGNA (FORLI)	DUSSELDORF (WEEZE)	HAMBURG (LUBECK)	LIMOGES	PALERMO	RIGA (GATEWAY TO LITHUANIA)	TOULON
ALICANTE	BRATISLAVA (VIENNA)	EINDHOVEN	HAUGESUND	LINZ	PALMA DE MALLORCA	ROME (CIAMPINO)	TOURS
ALTENBURG (LEIPZIG)	BREMEN	FRANKFURT (HAHN)	JEREZ	LODZ	PARMA	RZESZOW	TRIESTE
ANCONA	BRINDISI	FRIEDRICHSHAFEN	KARLSRUHE (BADEN-BADEN)	MARIBOR	PAU	SALZBURG	TURIN
BALATON	BRNO	GDANSK	KAUNAS	MARSEILLE (PROVENCE)	PERPIGNAN	SANTANDER (BILBAO)	VALENCIA
BARI	BYDGOSZCZ	GIRONA (BARCELONA)	KERRY	MILAN (BERGAMO)	PERUGIA	SANTIAGO DE COMPOSTELA	VALLADOLLID
BELFAST (CITY)	CARCASSONNE	GLASGOW (PRESTWICK)	KLAGENFURT	MONTPELLIER	PESCARA	SEVILLE	VENICE (TREVISO)
BERGERAC	CORK	GOTHENBURG (CITY)	KNOCK (IRELAND KNOCK WEST)	MURCIA	PISA (FLORENCE)	SHANNON	VERONA (BRESCIA)
BERLIN (SCHONEFELD)	DERRY	GRANADA	KRAKOW	NANTES	PORTO	STOCKHOLM (SKAVSTA & VASTERAS)	WROCLAW
BIARRITZ	DINARD	GRAZ	LAMEZIA	NEWQUAY	POZNAN	SZCZECIN	ZARAGOZA

TRAVEL FEB - MARCH '08

RYANAIR.COM

DISCOUNT HOTELS FROM ONLY £12 ON WWW.RYANAIRHOTELS.COM

Book until midnight tonight. Flights from London (Stansted), subject to availability, terms and conditions. See Ryanair.com for details.

at the farthest end, we built a small cubicle where liquid crystal was projected with a controlling system. The liquid crystal was heated systematically, and for the first time I had a liquid crystal projection, which was ceaseless, hour after hour. It worked quite well. Essentially that was the exhibition, with five or six exhibits.

Hans Ulrich Obrist — **The radical nature of your project reminds me of Alexander Dorner's credo that the museum or exhibition should be an interdisciplinary laboratory. In *The Way Beyond 'Art'*, Dorner wrote: 'The processual idea has penetrated our system of certainty [...] we cannot understand the forces which are effective in our visual production of today, if we do not have a look at other fields of modern life.'[14]**

Gustav Metzger — I appreciate all of that, and I was conscious that this was a radical departure, not just from my own practice but from art practice in general. If I can just add an art-historical note: there was an enormous discussion, and you can trace it in the literature, around 1966–67, where Anthony Caro and his students at Saint Martins were trying to liberate sculpture from the ground, to take it off the pedestal. One of the reasons I made this work was to prove the point that this is really off the ground, and I was very conscious of this connection with Saint Martins and other ideas in relation to sculpture. I feel I achieved something in that this was *literally* off the ground.

(14) Alexander Dorner, *The Way Beyond 'Art'. The Work of Herbert Bayer* (New York: Wittenborn, Schultz, 1947).

BOOK BY 13TH JANUARY!

The 2 Million seat NEW YEAR SALE!

FLY FROM £10 ONE WAY THIS SPRING & SUMMER!

	Travel 14.01.05 to 20.03.05	Travel 06.04.05 to 30.06.05
BIRMINGHAM TO:	from	from
Belfast City	£15	£19
Edinburgh	£12	£19
Glasgow Intl.	£15	£19
NEW! Malaga	-	£39
NEW! Alicante	-	£39
NEW! Murcia	-	£39
NEW! Palma	-	£39
NEW! Faro	-	£39
NEW! Almeria	-	£39
NEW! Brest Brittany	-	£34
NEW! Chambery	£59*	£59*
NEW! La Rochelle	-	£29
NEW! Bergerac	-	£29
NEW! Perpignan	-	£29
Toulouse	£29	£34
Salzburg	£59*	£59*
Shannon	£19	£29
LIVERPOOL TO:		
NEW! Southampton	-	£19
NEW! Edinburgh	-	£19
NEW! Glasgow Intl.	-	£19
NEW! Belfast City	£15	£19

	Travel 14.01.05 to 20.03.05	Travel 06.04.05 to 30.06.05
SOUTHAMPTON TO:	from	from
Edinburgh	£19	£25
NEW! Newcastle	£19	£19
NEW! Manchester	£15	£19
NEW! Glasgow Intl.	£19	£25
NEW! Brest Brittany	-	£34
NEW! Cherbourg	-	£19
NEW! Salzburg	£69*	£69*
Toulouse	£29	-
Bergerac	£29	£34
NEW! Chambery	£44†	£44†
NEW! Rennes	-	£29
NEW! Bordeaux	-	£29
NEW! Limoges	-	£29
NEW! Perpignan	-	£29
Belfast City	£19	£29
NEW! Geneva	£64**	£64**
Malaga	£39	£49
Alicante	£39	£49
Dublin	£24	£29
NEW! Murcia	£39	£49
NEW! La Rochelle	-	£34

	Travel 14.01.05 to 20.03.05	Travel 06.04.05 to 30.06.05
EXETER TO:	from	from
NEW! Paris	-	£29
NEW! Brest Brittany	-	£34
NEW! Liverpool	-	£19
NEW! Palma	-	£39
NEW! Newcastle	£15	£19
NEW! Faro	-	£49
Belfast City	£19	£25
Edinburgh	£19	£25
Glasgow Intl.	£19	£25
Malaga	£39	£49
Dublin	£24	£29
Alicante	£39	£49
LONDON GATWICK TO:		
Jersey	£24	£29
Guernsey	£24	£29
Belfast City	£19	£19
BELFAST CITY TO:		
NEW! Aberdeen	-	£19
Glasgow Intl.	£10	£19
Edinburgh	£10	£19
Newcastle	£10	£19

	Travel 14.01.05 to 20.03.05	Travel 06.04.05 to 30.06.05
LEEDS BRADFORD TO:	from	from
NEW! Southampton	-	£19
NEW! Exeter	-	£19
Belfast City	£10	£19
NORWICH TO:		
NEW! Glasgow Intl.	-	£25
NEW! Edinburgh	-	£25
NEW! Belfast City	£25	£25
NEW! Jersey	-	£39
JERSEY TO:		
NEW! London Southend	-	£59
NEW! Newcastle	-	£39
Birmingham	£24	£29
Southampton	£24	£29
Exeter	£24	£29
NEW! Bristol	-	£29
GUERNSEY TO:		
Birmingham	£29	£39
Southampton	£24	£29
Exeter	£24	£29
BRISTOL TO:		
Toulouse	£29	£34
Bordeaux	£29	£34
Belfast City	£12	£19
NEW! Bergerac	£29	£34

all fares are one way

flybe.com

british european

The backbone of UK travel.

3 DAYS FOR THE PRICE OF 2 ON CAR HIRE & HOTELS!

Fares are one way including taxes & charges, only available online, subject to availability. £1.75 handling fee applies to all credit cards & 40p for debit cards per passenger per one way flight. Restricted availability during peak holiday periods & major sporting events. 14 day advance purchase required. Start dates for new routes vary. *Saturdays only and operates until 16.04.05. **Operates until 18.04.05. †Operates until 17.04.05

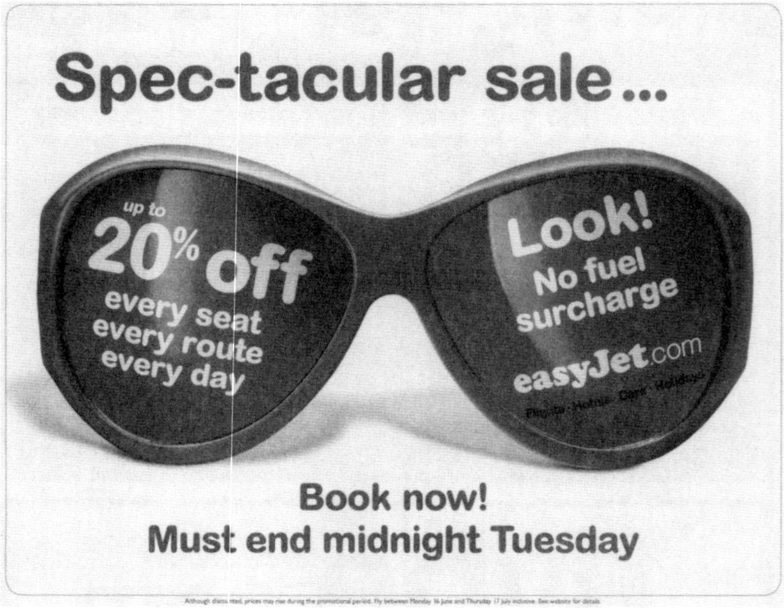
Spec-tacular sale...
up to
20% off
every seat
every route
every day
Look!
No fuel
surcharge
easyJet.com
Book now!
Must end midnight Tuesday
Although discounted, prices may rise during the promotional period. Fly between Monday 16 June and Thursday 17 July inclusive. See website for details.

III — Re-connection
Serpentine Gallery, London, June 2006

Hans Ulrich Obrist — We were talking about the exhibition in Lund ['Gustav Metzger. Works', Lunds Konsthall, 2006] and you told me about your new project.

Gustav Metzger — I remember. I think we might go back to the exhibition held at the Cubitt Gallery in the autumn of 2005. The work was entitled *Eichmann and the Angel*. On the very last day of the exhibition, Adam Szymczyk, the Director of Basel Kunsthalle, came by and more or less immediately decided to take it over.

Hans Ulrich Obrist — Can you tell me more about the show? Wasn't there a moveable structure?

Gustav Metzger — Yes, there was. The exhibition was based on a kind of reconstruction of the structure in which Eichmann was tried in Jerusalem in 1961. It wasn't a copy, but we came pretty close. So that was the central item, and then we had one wall, the end wall, literally covered with *The Guardian* newspaper, which was stacked. The third big element was a contraption—a metal rolling system used for rolling anything like boxes of beer or bundles of newspapers. So, visually, these were the three key elements. On one wall we had a reproduction of Paul Klee's angel.

Hans Ulrich Obrist — ***Angelus Novus.***

Gustav Metzger — Exactly—the work owned by Walter Benjamin. In fact, Walter Benjamin was at the centre of this whole concept. I felt the need to make a kind of homage to Benjamin and to the thousands and thousands of other Jews, exiles, intellectuals, musicians, and artists from Germany and Austria and wherever else in Europe they had to flee from. I had a very strong urge to do that, and so Benjamin became the centre of this entire concept. The other key figure is Hannah Arendt, who knew Benjamin and had manuscripts given to her by him. She wrote this major book, *Eichmann in Jerusalem*,[15] which as you know started out as five articles in *The New Yorker*. We had a table—a kind of reading area with one or two chairs where we had copied pages from the original publication of her articles in *The New Yorker*. It's quite impressive. Nobody has seen these articles except the people at the time of their publication.

(15) Hannah Arendt, *Eichmann in Jerusalem. A Report on the Banality of Evil* (London: Faber & Faber, 1963).

Hans Ulrich Obrist — **Did you have the original issues from back then?**

Gustav Metzger — We had photocopies of the opening pages of each article. On the left-hand wall, we had three texts starting with New York, and then Port Bou in the middle of the wall, and, towards the end, Jerusalem. So these are the places that are most relevant to the concept: New York, where Hannah Arendt lived and where she published these articles; Port Bou, where Benjamin died; and Jerusalem, where Eichmann was tried and eventually executed.

Hans Ulrich Obrist — **So it's very much an installation about displacement and place.**

Gustav Metzger — Yes, indeed. For me, the aim was to interlink these key elements and get as much meaning out of them in interaction and, again, in reference to Benjamin. In a key activity, we asked people to participate by going into what we called 'the cage', the structure in which Eichmann was tried. There was a chair in there and visitors could go in and sit down or stand. That was one interaction we offered to the public. In another activity, we invited people to take sheets of newspaper, put them on the roller, and let them roll along. The roller itself made a sort of humming noise, which to us was the noise of the carriages taking Jews to the concentration camps.

Hans Ulrich Obrist — **And that happened…**

Gustav Metzger — Continuously. The rollers were started when visitors arrived. As the newspapers rolled along, they would fall off and end up underneath the Klee image. At the end of the gallery, you had an impressive wall made up of *The Guardian* newspaper, and below Klee's angel, you had various newspapers in chaos.

Hans Ulrich Obrist — **Order and disorder.**

Gustav Metzger — Yes, those are some aspects.

Hans Ulrich Obrist — **This big installation, which was in Cubitt ['Eichmann and the Angel', Cubitt Gallery, London, 2005] and then in Basel ['Gustav Metzger. In Memoriam. New Works', Kunsthalle Basel, 2006], happened after your retrospective in Vienna ['Gustav Metzger. Geschichte Geschichte', Generali Foundation, Vienna, 2005].**

Gustav Metzger — Oh, yes, indeed. These were new works. The invitation came from the Curator at the time, David Bussell. I had a letter in late spring to do something for the autumn, and I had a wonderful collaboration with him and his gallery manager, Charlotte Nourse. So this Cubitt installation went to the Kunsthalle Basel, where it became part of a three-person exhibition. There was a young Palestinian photographer, Ahlam Shibli, and a young Cuban artist, Django Hernández, and so we shared the whole building. But when we started planning the exhibition, I was told there were two more rooms free for me to use, adjacent to the room that was suitable for *Eichmann and the Angel*. So I had a very short time to come up with an idea, and I thought I would never make it. One of these rooms is very big. It's on the ground floor, the end room, with top light—it's enormous. I started designing something based on a kind of Kleenex box, and I realised that this could be enlarged six times and we would end up with a very powerful form that connects with [Peter] Eisenman's work in Berlin. This linked in different ways with Eisenman's project.

Hans Ulrich Obrist — **It's a blow-up?**

Gustav Metzger — Yes. They ended up being 1.85 metres high. I went there and started working on this show for a few days. On the second day I was there, one young assistant was asked to enlarge the original, which she did within a few hours. It was absolutely amazing. It was a perfect form, and in cardboard, and the cardboard was ribbed, which reminded me of the grooves in Nazi architecture; the quality of the cardboard she had used reminded me immediately of the architecture of the Third Reich.

Hans Ulrich Obrist — **That was one of those incredible analogies, like *Après Paolozzi* [1997], which is a piece of foam plastic that looks similar to architecture.**

Gustav Metzger — I was completely knocked out, and so we decided that this was what we were going to do: we would fill these two rooms with these structures.

Hans Ulrich Obrist — **So it went from London to Basel. What is the link to Lund?**

Gustav Metzger — A Finnish curator you may know, Pontus Kyander, who lives in Lund, asked me for two years to work on an exhibition, which I was very reluctant to do. He used a bit of me in a BBC television film, and then wanted to arrange an exhibition of my work and of young artists who might relate to me in some way. Eventually we agreed that there would be a one-man show in the Konsthall in Lund. That's how it came about. Pontus came to the opening in Basel, by which time we had agreed to make an exhibition. I think he had already seen *Eichmann and the Angel* in London and wanted it for his exhibition. When he came to Basel and saw the other work with the 110 cardboard pieces, he said, 'We'll have that in Lund, as well.'

Hans Ulrich Obrist — **I heard you're also working on your unrealised documenta car [*KARBA*]. Basically, it involves the car being an anti-car monument.**

Gustav Metzger — That's in Lund now, yes. It's been realised already; he managed to do that. Are you familiar with the Konsthall?

Hans Ulrich Obrist — **Yes, I am.**

Gustav Metzger — Well, as you know, there's an open space in the middle. They built a three-metre cube there and just managed to put four cars around it. Once every hour, I believe, the motors start running automatically for one minute.

Hans Ulrich Obrist — **So the motor creates pollution?**

Gustav Metzger — Yes, but the pollution it creates is so minimal that it lasts for a mere minute and escapes at the top, where there are holes. The museum has discussed this with the health authorities, and they've agreed that it's not a problem. The people are usually in the gallery watching through the glass walls.

Hans Ulrich Obrist — **The cube becomes a smoking booth.**

Gustav Metzger — The fumes are pumped slowly, though of course in documenta the motors would have been running all day—that was the idea. So bit by bit works are being realised. Do you know a German critic called Eva Scharrer?

Hans Ulrich Obrist — **Yes, absolutely.**

Gustav Metzger — She came to the private view in Basel, and we happened to sit next to each other at dinner more or less by chance. There's always a big dinner at these events [*laughs*]. Soon after I returned to London, I got a letter from her telling me that the day after the private view, she received an invitation to become co-curator for the Sharjah Biennale, which she accepted. She immediately thought of putting on either the documenta piece or the piece with 120 cars there ['Stockholm June', 1972]. We've been in touch ever since, and she came to the private view in Lund. We've decided that we're going to do everything possible to bring the 120 cars to the Biennale, if only for a day.

Hans Ulrich Obrist — **How would this work with 120 cars? Can you describe it in greater detail?**

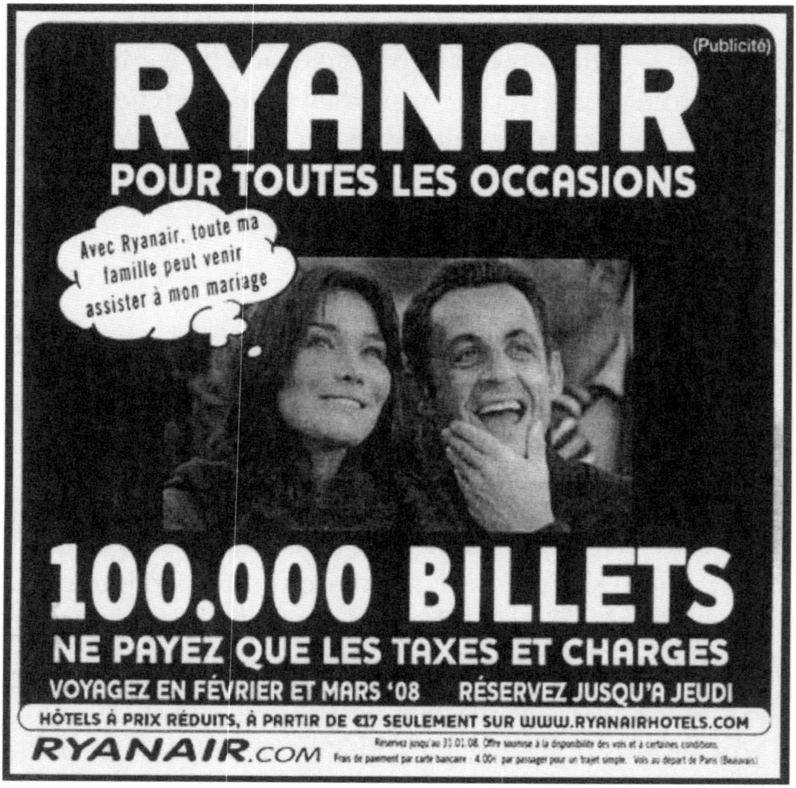
(Publicité)
RYANAIR
POUR TOUTES LES OCCASIONS
Avec Ryanair, toute ma famille peut venir assister à mon mariage
100.000 BILLETS
NE PAYEZ QUE LES TAXES ET CHARGES
VOYAGEZ EN FÉVRIER ET MARS '08
RÉSERVEZ JUSQU'A JEUDI
HÔTELS À PRIX RÉDUITS, À PARTIR DE €17 SEULEMENT SUR WWW.RYANAIRHOTELS.COM
RYANAIR.COM

Gustav Metzger — We would have a structure shaped like this, which would be big enough for thirty cars on each side. The structure would basically be made of metal rods or, as I now favour, pneumatic rods—rods where air is pumped in. Then we cover the structure with transparent plastic. However, it's all a question of getting permission. If we don't get permission to pump fumes into the structure, I would be quite happy if we built it and photographed it from the air with a helicopter. It would make amazing images. So that's what we're working on now. It's my biggest ongoing project.

Hans Ulrich Obrist — **It seems that the unrealised works you told me about in the last interview are becoming reality. Are there any unrealised works left? Do you still have big projects for the future?**

Gustav Metzger — [*laughs*] There are two other projects I'm working on that connect with Basel. I went to Basel twice and the Director said, 'Every so often we change the rear wall.' As you probably know, that wall is thirty-seven and a half metres long and five and a half metres high. He said, 'We're going to take this huge composition based on ceramic plates off, and we want you to make a proposal to fill that wall.' So again I went back to London, started designing the wall, and submitted a proposal. I did this all very quickly. My proposal, which has been accepted by Basel Kunsthalle, is to use refrigerators and put them on the wall to indicate the loss of the ozone layer through the chemicals that are expelled from them.

Hans Ulrich Obrist — So it's a chemical focus, basically.

Gustav Metzger — Yes, the chemicals that are taken out or not taken out. The project is fairly simple, and it should be straightforward because I want young people to understand it without too much difficulty.

Hans Ulrich Obrist — I remember when you came to see me exactly eleven years ago at the Serpentine Gallery during 'Take me (I'm yours)' and somebody said, 'Mr. Metzger is downstairs.' So I went downstairs and we met in the exhibition. You told me that you had also done things at the Goethe Institute.

Gustav Metzger — Yes.

Hans Ulrich Obrist — But are they in the Generali Foundation book?[16] I couldn't find them here. [*Picks up the book and begins paging through it*]

Gustav Metzger — It's in there somewhere.

Hans Ulrich Obrist — What year was the '3 Life Situations' exhibition?

Gustav Metzger — It was in the spring of '72. There's a reference. Everything, practically, is referred to in this book. It's an amazing production.

Hans Ulrich Obrist — What did you do at the Goethe Institute exactly?

Gustav Metzger — It was an exhibition of three artists who were invited to open that building ['3 Life Situations',

(16) Sabine Breitwieser (ed.), *Gustav Metzger. Geschichte Geschichte*, exh. cat. Generali Foundation, Vienna (Ostfildern-Ruit: Hatje Cantz, 2005).

Gallery House, London, 1972]. The building wasn't derelict, but it hadn't been used, so it was all dusty. There was Marc Chaimowicz, Stuart Brisley, and me, and we were to open up this building.

Hans Ulrich Obrist — **It doesn't show a picture of what you did.**

Gustav Metzger — No. Each of us was given a floor. Stuart Brisley was on the ground floor, and he did one of his key works, sitting in the dark for weeks, and Marc Chaimowicz had the beautiful kind of ballroom, which he has since re-created, in the Migros Museum in Zürich, for example.

Hans Ulrich Obrist — **I saw that last weekend, yes.**

Gustav Metzger — I had the second floor, which was different to the others. The others were large rooms, but on the second floor there was an apartment. It had a room, another room, a bathroom and a kitchen, and then two more rooms. I decided to use all these rooms for different purposes. In the first room I had the model with 120 cars—the one that's going to be realised now in Sharjah. In the next room there were realised and unrealised projects. These were large photomontages made by a young German artist who was studying at the Slade [School of Fine Art, London].

Hans Ulrich Obrist — **Was that the *Monument to Bloody Sunday* [London, 1972]?**

Gustav Metzger — Yes, and the side wall of the Royal Festival Hall for liquid crystals and floating metal on the

Thames. Are they all in the book? Are they listed there? Tell us what it says.

Hans Ulrich Obrist — **Yes. It says, 'Projects Realised I (Monument to Bloody Sunday) shows a large building opposite the Institute of Contemporary Art in London, which Gustav Metzger declares to be a monument for Bloody Sunday in Northern Ireland'.[17] So that was a readymade.**

Gustav Metzger — No.

Hans Ulrich Obrist — **It existed, it was realised.**

Gustav Metzger — But the realisation is the turning round of its function, as it were. This was a kind of war cabinet, a top-secret British institution, and I turned it around into something that would be completely unacceptable to the establishment. By the way, this was made almost immediately after Bloody Sunday; it wasn't a historical look back to Bloody Sunday on January 30, 1972. It was hot in the news when I presented it in the spring.

Hans Ulrich Obrist — **'Project Unrealised concerns the project Gustav Metzger presented unsuccessfully to the Greater London Council in 1971.'[18] So these are the unrealised projects.**

Gustav Metzger — That's right. One involved a piece of metal that would float on the Thames in front of the National Film Theatre, going up and down with the water. At night it would be lit up and would reflect the light. Then there was another project, again in front of the

(17) Sabine Breitwieser (ed.), *Gustav Metzger. Geschichte Geschichte*, exh. cat. Generali Foundation, Vienna (Ostfildern-Ruit: Hatje Cantz, 2005), p. 164.
(18) Ibid.

National Film Theatre, the space where the book dealers now stand. Well, I proposed a huge cube of newspapers that would start on the ground underneath Waterloo Bridge and would build up to a solid mass of papers, and hit Waterloo Bridge. All these projects were rejected. The two projects on GLC ground were rejected, except for the floating metal. They said, 'If you can get permission from Trinity House, you can do it.' And I got permission, but it was never realised. Anyhow, that was in 1971.

Hans Ulrich Obrist — **In another room, visitors were welcome to use the kitchen, where food and drink was available. But what about the bathroom?**

Gustav Metzger — The bathroom was actually the most interesting part. I spent some time thinking about the bathroom, which needed a good clean. So I decided to clean it and offer it to the public as a venue. I put up a small notice on paper: 'You are free to use this bathroom. Ask for towels downstairs.' At least one person actually did use it. Of course, it was a splendid house, and the bathroom was beautiful after I had cleaned it, especially the mirror. I was after a total experience. It wasn't just a matter of offering people the chance to have a clean-up, but to experience the aesthetics of hot water and steam on the mirror and in the room as a whole. This relates to 'Manifesto World' of 1962, which says that everything, everything, everything can be responded to as art—can be apprehended as art.[19] So that bathroom is, for me, a kind of fulfilment of the '62 manifesto ten years before.

(19) 'Manifesto World', Fourth Manifesto, typescript (London, 1962).

Hans Ulrich Obrist — It was a big show because then there was also *Controlling Information from Below.*

Gustav Metzger — That was the last room.

Hans Ulrich Obrist — Where 'SMASH IT' was written on the wall. That also anticipates 'Take Me (I'm Yours)' [Serpentine Gallery, 1995]. But how did it work with the newspapers? Could people make their own newspaper or the 'SMASH IT' thing?

Gustav Metzger — No, 'SMASH IT' was just a statement on the system—smash the system.

Hans Ulrich Obrist — Could visitors make their own collages?

[*Julia Peyton-Jones enters*]

Gustav Metzger — They could, but as it turned out, members of the public hardly came in. As you know, exhibitions are mostly not inhabited by visitors.

Julia Peyton-Jones — *In the seventies, absolutely not—maybe two or three a week.*

Gustav Metzger — We didn't get many visitors. I spent quite a bit of time there, and we talked—the artists talked. We had to clean the place out, and there was trouble with Sigi Krauss. The name may be unfamiliar to you. He was in charge of the house. We never saw him, not even once. His assistant was Rosetta Brooks. She came in and did some work, but not very much. At one point, we thought we would strike and just stop the whole thing. Things were getting so bad in terms

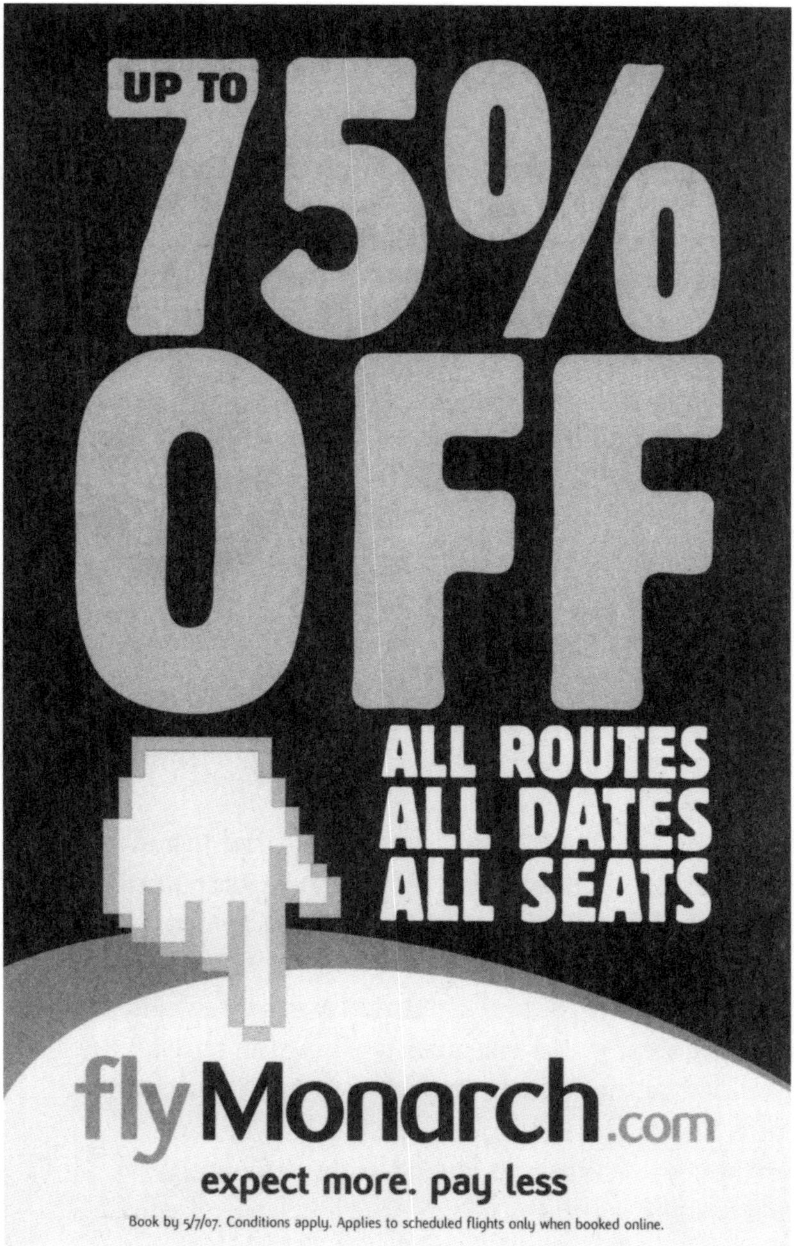
UP TO
75%
OFF
ALL ROUTES
ALL DATES
ALL SEATS
flyMonarch.com
expect more. pay less
Book by 5/7/07. Conditions apply. Applies to scheduled flights only when booked online.

of organisation. That would also help explain why we had so few visitors. They just didn't work on it; it's very sad. The Goethe Institute had nothing to say because they had delegated authority to Sigi Krauss.

Julia Peyton-Jones — *It's so interesting to have one of those houses really unoccupied, except by artists. Hans Ulrich and I have talked a lot about the fact that the Serpentine is a house—and very much about the Serpentine's role in this incredibly dynamic and hugely changed cultural landscape. Here, I mean culture in the widest sense, also in terms of how people live. We also discuss what singles us out from other institutions. In any case, that idea of artists inhabiting the house is very interesting, and this seems to be what you did.*

Gustav Metzger — That was the idea, to live there. Marc and Stuart lived there as much as possible, though I didn't because I was preparing an exhibition at the AA, the Architectural Association.

Hans Ulrich Obrist — It was called 'Unrealisable Disintegrative Architecture' ['Unrealisable Disintegrative Architecture and Other Projects', Architectural Association, London, 1972].

Gustav Metzger — Yes, exactly. While I was in Gallery House and preparing it, I was also working on the AA, so I couldn't actually have stayed.

Hans Ulrich Obrist — What did you do at the AA?

Gustav Metzger — It was a relatively small exhibition, and unfortunately I can hardly remember it in detail. There were some models, but there was also a lecture, which was perhaps more important for me than the exhibition. It was a minor thing, though, only lasting about two weeks. Does it give the dates?

Hans Ulrich Obrist — It just says it was a short show and that there was a lecture. There's an interesting plan here. It says *KARBA* is a metallic frame with plastic, two and a half metres, and four cars.

Gustav Metzger — Is that plan in the context of the AA?

Hans Ulrich Obrist — No, that's documenta.

Gustav Metzger — As I said, it was a minor thing.

Hans Ulrich Obrist — Returning for a moment to the Gallery House, we spoke the other day with Damien Hirst about [Kurt] Schwitters. I was wondering if Schwitters and the *Merzbau* played a role for you.

Gustav Metzger — The influence is quite clear: there were two Schwitters exhibitions in Lords Gallery, in 1958 and 1959, and I went to both. Each of them was a very, very important experience for me. Of course, '59 was the year I moved out of painting, so there's no question that these two Schwitters exhibitions were significant. Naturally, I knew Schwitters before these exhibitions, but to actually see fine examples of his work was special, and this was in a private house.

Julia Peyton-Jones — *What a privilege!*

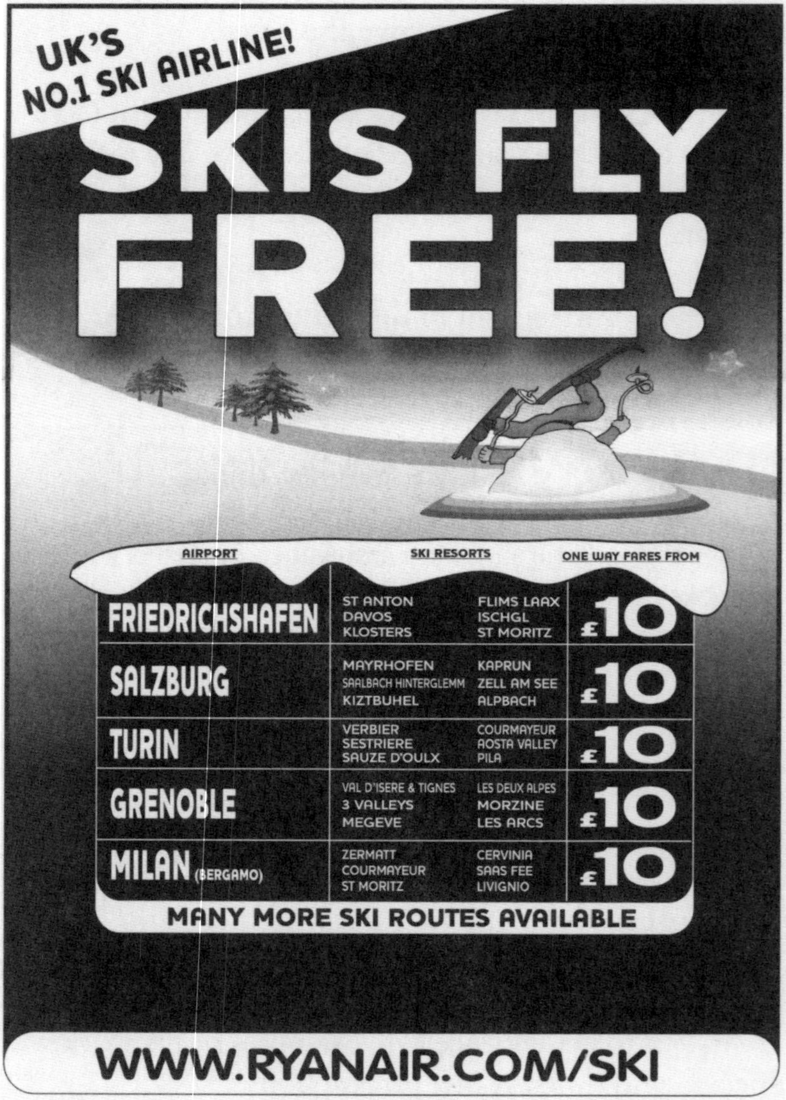

Fares valid until midnight 27.09.07. Subject to availability, terms & conditions. Flights direct from London (Stansted). Passengers must book by 30th Sept '07 to avail of the skis for free offer. Terms & conditions apply.

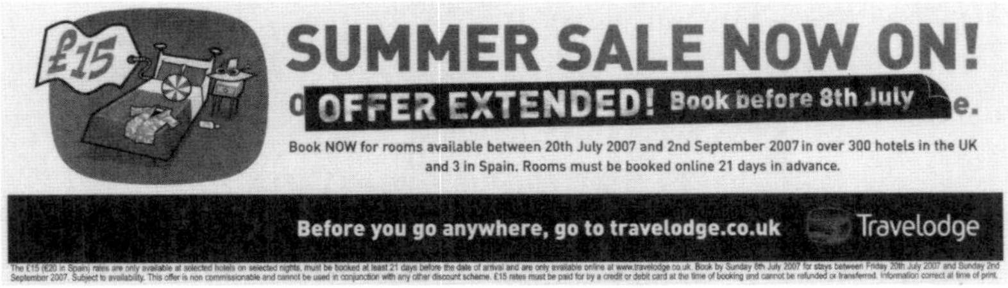
£15
SUMMER SALE NOW ON!
OFFER EXTENDED! Book before 8th July
Book NOW for rooms available between 20th July 2007 and 2nd September 2007 in over 300 hotels in the UK and 3 in Spain. Rooms must be booked online 21 days in advance.
Before you go anywhere, go to travelodge.co.uk
Travelodge
The £15 (€20 in Spain) rates are only available at selected hotels on selected nights, must be booked at least 21 days before the date of arrival and are only available online at www.travelodge.co.uk. Book by Sunday 8th July 2007 for stays between Friday 20th July 2007 and Sunday 2nd September 2007. Subject to availability. This offer is non commissionable and cannot be used in conjunction with any other discount scheme. £15 rates must be paid for by a credit or debit card at the time of booking and cannot be refunded or transferred. Information correct at time of print.

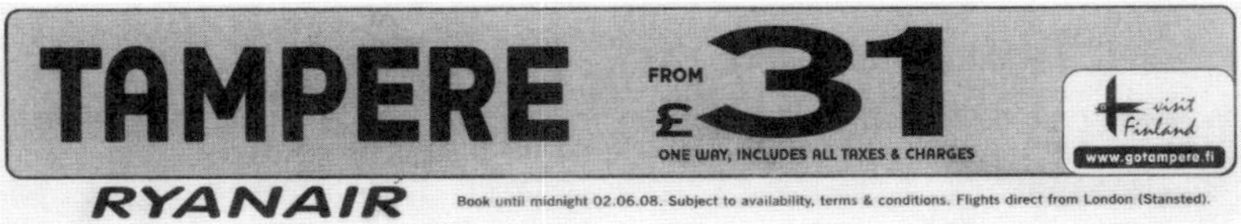
TAMPERE
FROM £31
ONE WAY, INCLUDES ALL TAXES & CHARGES
visit Finland
www.gotampere.fi
RYANAIR
Book until midnight 02.06.08. Subject to availability, terms & conditions. Flights direct from London (Stansted).

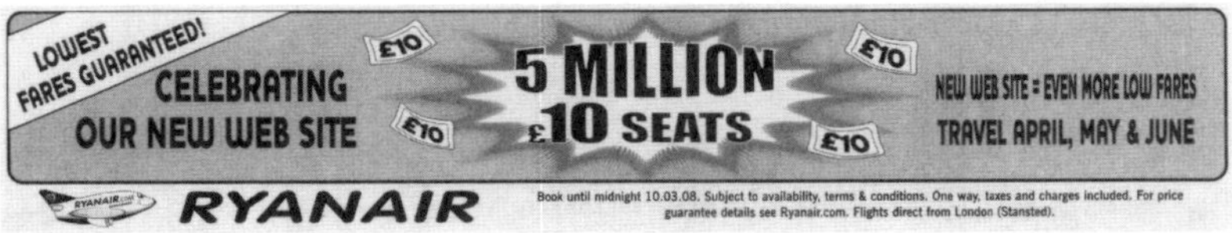
LOWEST FARES GUARANTEED!
CELEBRATING OUR NEW WEB SITE
£10
5 MILLION
£10 SEATS
NEW WEB SITE = EVEN MORE LOW FARES
TRAVEL APRIL, MAY & JUNE
RYANAIR
Book until midnight 10.03.08. Subject to availability, terms & conditions. One way, taxes and charges included. For price guarantee details see Ryanair.com. Flights direct from London (Stansted).

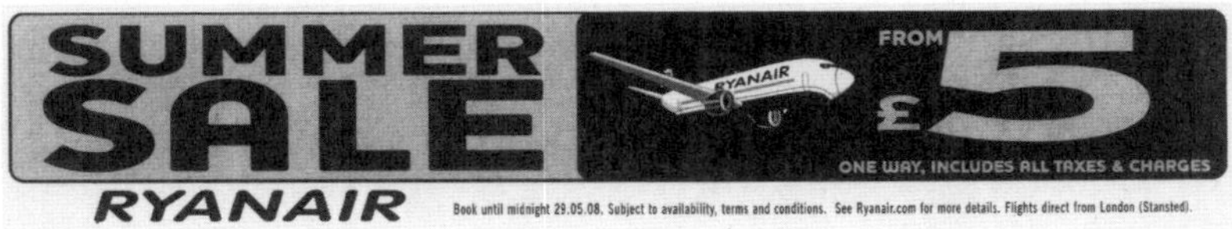
SUMMER SALE
FROM £5
ONE WAY, INCLUDES ALL TAXES & CHARGES
RYANAIR
Book until midnight 29.05.08. Subject to availability, terms and conditions. See Ryanair.com for more details. Flights direct from London (Stansted).

Gustav Metzger — It was in Philip Granville's house—a private house functioning as a gallery.

Hans Ulrich Obrist — **But you never met Schwitters.**

Gustav Metzger — No.

Julia Peyton-Jones — *Gentlemen, may I interrupt you for a second? I unfortunately have to go to a meeting.*

[*Julia Peyton-Jones leaves*]

Hans Ulrich Obrist — **Where were we? You were speaking about the wall at the Basel Kunsthalle.**

Gustav Metzger — The design goes like this: we'll start on the left side of the wall with one line of refrigerators, and then we'll have three or four refrigerators that will be attached to the wall above or below each other like this, and they'll be at an angle.

Hans Ulrich Obrist — **They'll be slanted.**

Gustav Metzger — Slanted, yes. Then about five metres further along, we'll have two lines of refrigerators, and so we'll end up with five sets of refrigerators next to and below each other. Then, on top of the first, next to the first line of refrigerators, we'll have a disc made of reflective metal to indicate the sun—the sun's heat, and changes in its intensity. At each step, the sun goes down, down, down until it reaches the bottom of the last set of refrigerators. The idea, again, is our changing relationship to the sun; the more refrigerators and the more chemicals we use, the more the sun's heat changes in relation to the earth. That's the principle.

Hans Ulrich Obrist — **Very interesting. So that will be realised this year.**

Gustav Metzger — We hope so; we're certainly working towards that this year.

Hans Ulrich Obrist — **To come back for a second to Schwitters...**

Gustav Metzger — Sure.

Hans Ulrich Obrist — **There's a direct link from Schwitters to your early cardboard works.**

Gustav Metzger — Direct.

Hans Ulrich Obrist — **Even now there's often a link to Schwitters in your work. We've never spoken about why Schwitters and the *Merzbau* are important to you or about the idea of the *Merzbau* as a shrine of friendship.**

Gustav Metzger — Frankly, I'm far more interested in his collages. I've never seen the *Merzbau* in the north of England. I should have seen it by now. I've only seen reproductions of the earlier one that was destroyed. But Dada and surrealism and constructivism and futurism—all the 'isms'—are also elements I came onto when I was very young, especially when I arrived in London. I would have been nineteen at the time, so I immediately started going round the art bookshops in Charing Cross Road and buying books. I had very little money, but back then you could buy Wyndham Lewis publications for one shilling. Zwemmers had a cellar with hundreds of them, which were beginning to... not rot, but they had become damp, so they were being sold for a shilling.

Hans Ulrich Obrist — **What interested you about Wyndham Lewis? Was it the idea of the manifesto? It was a moment when many artists were producing manifestos.**

Gustav Metzger — I was certainly interested in the Vorticist Manifesto. It's important to remember that [David] Bomberg, who became my teacher in the autumn of 1945 just a few months after I came to study in London, knew Wyndham Lewis. He would tell us stories. Wyndham Lewis, he would tell us, was a bit of an anti-Semite, and so was [French sculptor Henri] Gaudier-Brzeska in particular. In fact, there was a real fight between Gaudier-Brzeska and Bomberg, which actually became physical at some point—some kind of fight. That's one reason for my interest. Bomberg himself was avant-garde. He was, at a very early age, a leading figure in the British avant-garde, and of course he remained interested in all that. So there was a direct link between the pre-First World War and post-World War through Bomberg. Bomberg would tell us stories about these people and was particularly fond of telling us how Wyndham Lewis had wanted him to sign the Vorticist Manifesto and Bomberg refused.

Hans Ulrich Obrist — **The early twentieth-century avant-garde was also the avant-garde related to utopias, and I think your generation had a very different relationship to utopias than** someone in the 1920s. Could you talk a little bit about your relationship to utopia? I'm curious, because you participated in 'Utopia Station' at the Venice Biennale in 2003.[20]

Gustav Metzger — As you know, I wanted to become a revolutionary at the age of eighteen. I seriously considered it from the age of seventeen and, well, that's utopia, isn't it? Rightly or wrongly, as we know looking back on it, that was definitely utopia. Change the world, yes?

Hans Ulrich Obrist — A kind of anarchist utopia?

Gustav Metzger — I was more of a communist, and Lenin was the key figure for me. At the time, I would have been a communist revolutionary rather than an anarchist revolutionary. I lived in a community in Bristol where you had Trotskyites and anarchists, who were close to communists. That was in 1944 for six or seven months, and it was there that I realised that utopia wasn't for me. So I chose the way of art and sculpture. It was a clear decision. I had to make a choice, and in the late summer I made that choice. But for me art would turn out to be a continuation of the political ideals I had around the age of sixteen, seventeen, and eighteen. It wasn't that I abandoned the idea of change. I wanted to change the world, to change art; I wanted to work in art to make changes of some kind.

Hans Ulrich Obrist — How would you define utopia now? Ernst Bloch, when he was pushed against the wall by Adorno to define utopia, said, 'Something is missing.' The whole notion

(20) 'Utopia Station' at the Venice Biennale 2003, co-curated by Molly Nesbit, Hans Ulrich Obrist, and Rirkrit Tiravanija.

of utopia being defined as something missing is fascinating. What would your definition of utopia be?

Gustav Metzger — I will be quite frank with you. It's not a concept that I'm concerned with. I'm concerned with the ongoing discussion. I read a fair amount—not so much books anymore, but papers, and I listen to discussions on the radio where these subjects come up on the third programme. On *Night Waves* [BBC Radio 3], for example, you get this again and again on art and politics, so I follow the discussion. I'm very interested in this. But for me, utopia is a foreign word, and I'm quite frankly suspicious of its use. We've been knocked on the head so many times now, we've been disillusioned, we've gone the wrong way, we've followed paths that didn't go anywhere, and so we've had our fingers burnt in relation to utopia. I try not to use the word. I felt very hesitant before taking part in the Venice Biennale utopia project for these reasons.

Hans Ulrich Obrist — **Maybe you can tell me about the image you submitted. It was a kind of destroyed archive—part of the 100,000 newspapers installation, wasn't it? It went to Lyon afterwards [Biennale d'Art Contemporain, Lyon, 2003].**

Gustav Metzger — That's right. In the strangest way, the image actually does relate to utopia, because you have chaos, and if you'd been in that installation, you would have seen that the chaos was far greater than what you see here. There were piles of things disintegrating within the installation, newspapers almost turning to dust. It's this twisting form that relates to utopia—this turning in on itself and going up into the future, so it's like a finger pointing into the future. This is the most amazing photograph, but it was an extraordinary set-up.

Hans Ulrich Obrist — **The show was *100,000 Newspapers* [2002–03], wasn't it?**

Gustav Metzger — Yes. We didn't have that many papers, but we had at least ten thousand.

Hans Ulrich Obrist — **But you have many newspapers, haven't you?**

Gustav Metzger — I haven't bought as many these last two years, because I bought so many before.

Hans Ulrich Obrist — **It's your own archive and not an installation, isn't it?**

Gustav Metzger — It could be seen as an archive; it's an accumulation. One day I might exhibit it.

Hans Ulrich Obrist — **I'd like to talk more about London, which has played a very big role in your work. You've lived here ever since you first came to England.**

Gustav Metzger — London has always fascinated me. It's the most important city for me. I first came here as a twelve-year-old child. It was in 1939, towards the end of January, I think, and I lived here till the outbreak of the war. During the war, I lived in different places, including Cambridge, where my brother, Max/Mendel, and I started our studies at the Cambridge School of Art. In September 1945 we returned to London together and immediately took up residence in the

East End, which seemed the right place to us. We had joined the Sir John Cass Institute at Aldgate for our sculpture studies, so it made perfect sense to live as closely as we could to the school, at Aldgate East.

Hans Ulrich Obrist — **Have you lived in London ever since?**

Gustav Metzger — With interruptions, of course.

Hans Ulrich Obrist — **London comes up a lot in your work. It pops up in your works and in the newspapers, because most of the newspapers are from London; it pops up in your archives and in your unrealised projects; and it also pops up in videos like *Power to the People* ['Independence', South London Gallery, London, 2003].**

Gustav Metzger — Yes indeed. London has this unbelievable potential; wherever you go, there's something you can research, something you can study.

Hans Ulrich Obrist — **Bomberg struggled with the question of how to portray the city, and it's something that [Oskar] Kokoschka also dealt with, but in a very different way. Obviously, it's impossible for a painter to make a synthetic portrait of a city; it always changes. What's your take on the idea of making a portrait of a city?**

Gustav Metzger — It's just packed, isn't it? Now, especially, it's becoming more significant in terms of the visual arts. I met two members of the [Centre] Pompidou staff on Sunday—a man and a woman. I don't know them, but the woman said they had just spent the day in London at the National Gallery, the Victoria and Albert

Museum, and Tate Modern. She said, 'It's unbelievable—it's so much better than Paris in every sense. The feeling, the people, what we saw.' I was very surprised to hear this coming from a staff member of the Pompidou.

Hans Ulrich Obrist — **This notion of a packed city is very interesting. You made this piece called *Power to the People* in 2003. Can you tell me about it?**

Gustav Metzger — It was quite an extraordinary event. The war had just been declared.

Hans Ulrich Obrist — **On Iraq.**

Gustav Metzger — Yes. I was in the city, as I often am, in the area near Trafalgar Square. Actually, I was in the Strand and I saw young people coming towards me, almost marching, from the East. I asked what was going on, and they replied, 'We're going to a demo at Parliament Square.' They had left school and were going to this demo. I thought, 'Well, I've got a few more things to do. I'll go and look at it when I'm finished.' So I finished my errands, and between twelve and one I arrived at the demonstration. I was amazed by what I saw—hundreds and hundreds of these young people. I went back the next day to see it again. That day there was a turning point, when the young people rushed into the street, occupying it. I'll make a quick diagram: here's Parliament Square, here's Parliament, and here's the statue of Churchill. This is the corner where young people occupied the street, or bits of the street anyway. There's a road here, and exactly opposite

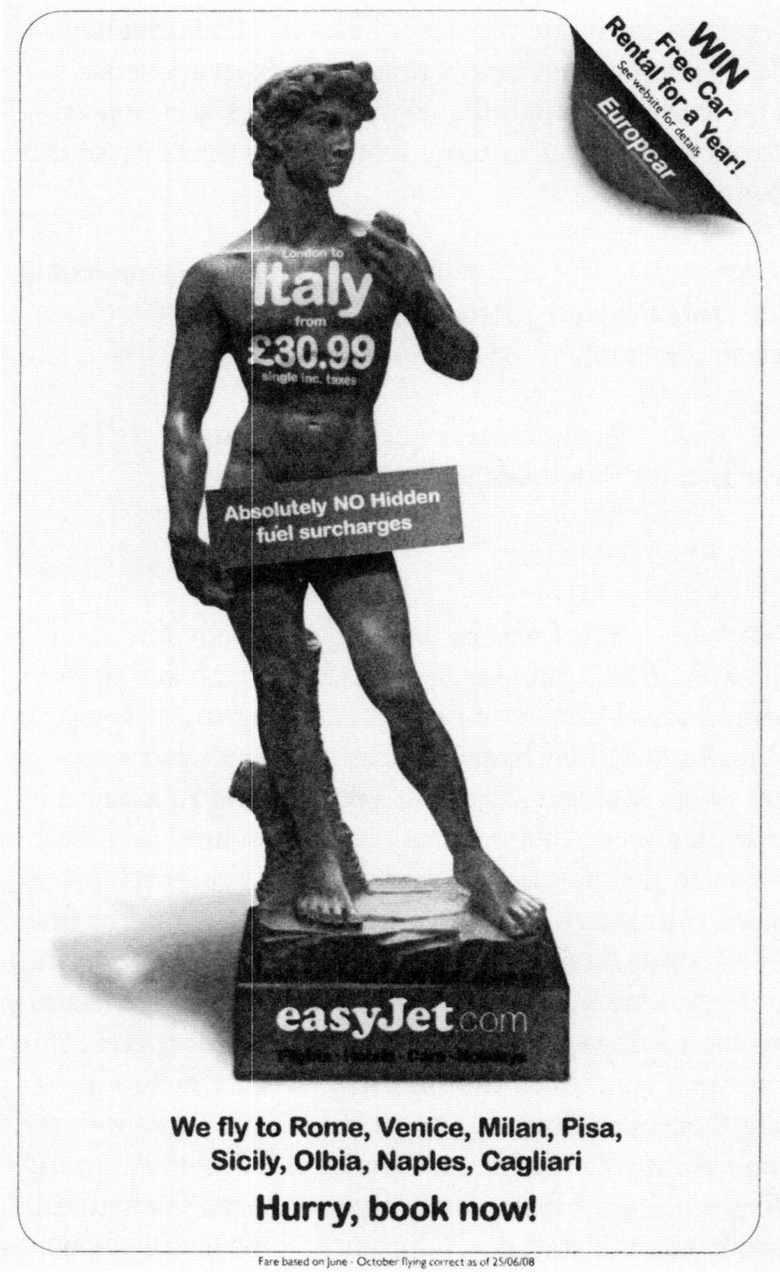
WIN
Free Car
Rental for a Year!
See website for details
Europcar
London to
Italy
from
£30.99
single inc. taxes
Absolutely NO Hidden
fuel surcharges
easyJet.com
We fly to Rome, Venice, Milan, Pisa,
Sicily, Olbia, Naples, Cagliari
Hurry, book now!
Fare based on June - October flying correct as of 25/06/08

the area they were occupying was the Ministry of Defence, where in 1961 Bertrand Russell, with the Committee of 100—including me—staged our first sit-down. So for me, this juxtaposition was unbelievable: the fact that we had been there, demonstrating against a similar issue, against war, in February 1961. Then a woman, about thirty years old, came with a megaphone and began to chant, 'Power to the people!' And everyone sitting there began to chant, 'The people have the power. The people have the power. *Power. Power. Power.*' This went on for about twenty minutes or more. It was an unbelievable experience. I was incredibly moved.

Hans Ulrich Obrist — Did you film it?

Gustav Metzger — No, I didn't, but that's how the video originated—from those two days. I was invited, at very short notice, to contribute to the 'Independence' exhibition at the South London Gallery [2003], and I initially wasn't sure what to contribute. Then I realised that I could make the video. One of the organisers of the exhibition, Chris Hammond, actually did the work on the video and helped to find material. We couldn't find the sound to 'Power to the people', but we found some videos of the sit-down and demonstrations.

Hans Ulrich Obrist — Another way the city enters your work is obviously through the newspaper. I've always been very fascinated by the *Evening Standard* posters, because for me they're London.

Gustav Metzger — The title of that series is 'London a.m., London p.m.' [2005]. I've made a number of pieces like this. The idea is that you get the first edition in the morning and another edition in the afternoon, and sometimes there's more than two. I'm now speaking of the past, because the paper has changed a bit, but in the old days the first edition simply had the top line blank and the later editions would have 'West End Final'. So there's a graphic difference. I decided to make a series of works where you have the morning edition, which had nothing on top, and next to it, on the left, the poster. And then, on the right you have the latest edition, 'West End Final', with a different poster. This is the idea that's been exhibited at the Generali Foundation.

Hans Ulrich Obrist — **What would be your advice for the upcoming Serpentine Marathon?**

Gustav Metzger — You really should try and get Tom McCarthy. I don't know if you know him.

Hans Ulrich Obrist — **He's a brilliant writer.**

Gustav Metzger — He did a work on London recently at Beaconsfield [Gallery]. It's a brilliant piece. Someone you should certainly contact is Lisa Jardine, a professor at Queen Mary College, University of London. She's really involved in London; she recently did a series of ten-minute talks on Sunday mornings before the Nine O'Clock News.

Hans Ulrich Obrist — **Does she teach?**

Gustav Metzger — Oh yes. She's Professor of Renaissance Studies, but she's also a kind of universal figure. She's the daughter of Jacob Bronowski, and she organises the annual Bronowski Lectures at the university. I was there a few weeks ago when [Melvyn] Bragg was the speaker. Lisa Jardine is totally obsessed with London and knows everything about it, and she's a very fine speaker. She will agree; she likes to communicate. David King is another possibility; he has an archive of Russian communism. He's very good.

Hans Ulrich Obrist — **We also thought of Tony Benn.**

Gustav Metzger — Tony Benn, definitely. And [Eric] Hobsbawm, of course, would be one of the best people you could get.

Hans Ulrich Obrist — **I've interviewed him. He said we need a protest against forgetting.**

Gustav Metzger — Alistair Campbell, and [Neil] McGregor, the Director of the British Museum. Of course, he'll know his London. What about Pete Townshend? He's travelling a lot now with the band, or was going to, so I think you should get a hold of him as early as possible. But he'd be very good.

Hans Ulrich Obrist — **You worked with him in the sixties, didn't you?**

Gustav Metzger — Yes, I did. Will this be on video as well?

Hans Ulrich Obrist — **Yes, it will be documented and then it will be transcribed.**

Gustav Metzger — And published as a book?

Hans Ulrich Obrist — Yes.

Gustav Metzger — Good God! That's a very big project.

Hans Ulrich Obrist — It is indeed! Gustav, I think that's more or less what I wanted to ask you for today. It's been a fantastic new chapter in our evolving interview, which we will definitely continue in July. Now that we're in the same city, I hope our meetings will be more frequent. It would be really nice.

Gustav Metzger — I hope so, too. If you want a good Indian restaurant, then I recommend *Chowki*, on Denman Street; it's a good-looking restaurant and it's very reasonable. If you go there, especially in the afternoon, it's almost completely empty and they serve all day. It's a good place to meet for a quiet talk.

Hans Ulrich Obrist — Let's try to do our next interview there.

Gustav Metzger — Yes, let's do that.

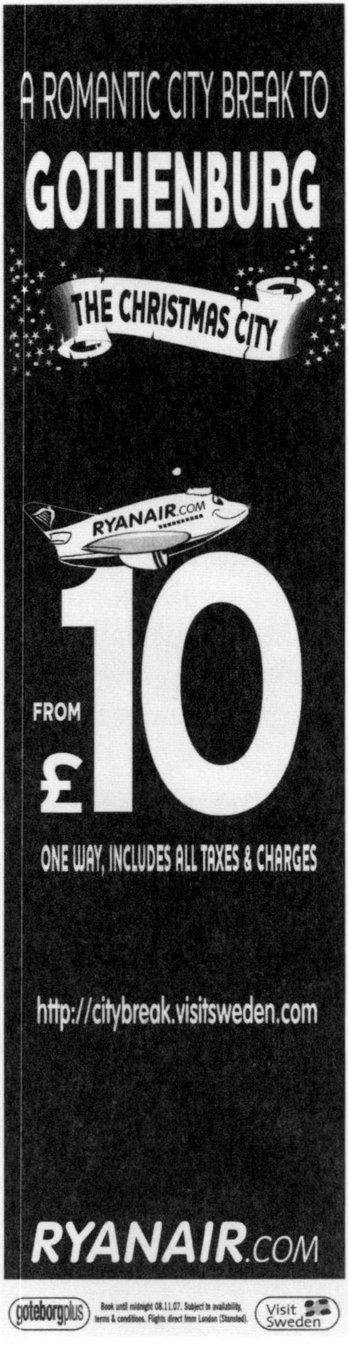
A ROMANTIC CITY BREAK TO
GOTHENBURG
THE CHRISTMAS CITY
RYANAIR.COM
FROM
£10
ONE WAY, INCLUDES ALL TAXES & CHARGES
http://citybreak.visitsweden.com
RYANAIR.COM
goteborgplus
Book until midnight 08.11.07. Subject to availability, terms & conditions. Flights direct from London (Stansted).
Visit Sweden

IV — Marathon
Serpentine Gallery, London, July 28–29, 2006

Hans Ulrich Obrist — It's a great pleasure to introduce our next guest, Gustav Metzger!

[*applause*]

Hans Ulrich Obrist — Gustav Metzger is one of the only guests at our Marathon who has actually been here from the very first moment.

Rem Koolhaas — *That's why everyone is applauding!*

Hans Ulrich Obrist — One of the first times we talked was at Café Cosmo at Waterloo. We had a conversation there, during which you told me about your long relationship to London, about your arrival as a refugee, and about your studies with David Bomberg. Could you tell us how it all started in London—about your beginnings in London, and perhaps about Bomberg?

Gustav Metzger — My first contact with Great Britain was arriving at Harwich from Holland by boat with 500 other refugee children, including my elder brother, Max/Mendel. After a few weeks on the coast, we were transported to London by bus. My first experience of London was thousands of car lights as we passed through the traffic, something I had never seen before, coming from the relatively small town of Nuremberg. The next strong memory I'd like to talk about was that every Sunday evening a bus would pull up in front of our hostel in Kilburn, and twenty or so refugee children and youths would be transported to the grandest cinema in London—the Gaumont State Theatre in Kilburn. We were given the best central balcony seats with compliments from the manager. So these are the first memories. Some months after the end of the war, we both came back to London and continued with our studies. That went on for seven or eight years.

Hans Ulrich Obrist — It would be good to hear more about Bomberg, because we've heard a lot about...

Rem Koolhaas — *... schools.*

Hans Ulrich Obrist — Schools—about memory and also about transmission. Please tell us more about Bomberg and about your dialogue with him.

Gustav Metzger — Again, let me start with my first impression. We had problems finding enough life classes to complete our studies. So in the end, my brother and I had four classes, including one, I think, in Hammersmith. The problem was the heating in the life classes at that time of scarcity. So I remember walking into the life room, and there was a small man who looked sort of unprepossessing. It was David Bomberg. But within a few weeks one realised that this was not an ordinary person. He was charismatic, he had enormous experience, and he was, I think, a great artist. He did his utmost to teach everyone, literally everyone, in that thirteen-, fourteen-strong class. Whatever was possible. And for many years after 1945, I would attend his classes. At the end, he had evening classes only, from '50 to '53. I lived outside London much of the time and had to travel in just for the two hours of study with him. I can't be more positive about Bomberg. But whatever I say about him, it can't possibly convey the level of significance he had for me and for so many others.

Rem Koolhaas — *I understand that you were a member of Fluxus, of sorts. Were you an official or an unofficial member?*

Gustav Metzger — Actually, this is a bit of a misunderstanding. The essential facts. In 1962 the artists [Daniel] Spoerri and [Robert] Filliou were invited by Victor Musgrave to organise an exhibition in London ['Festival of Misfits']. This was at Gallery One in October 1962. Ben Vautier, Arthur Koepcke, and Robin Page participated in the exhibition. Eventually, there were four or five people who would be going into Fluxus. Fluxus barely existed at that point—certainly not in England. Since I took part in the exhibition indirectly—and definitely took part in an evening at the ICA, where we were joined by Dick Higgins and his wife Alison Knowles, who were absolutely Fluxus at that time—it has been said that this evening was the very first Fluxus event in England. That's quite acceptable.

Hans Ulrich Obrist — You've written your own manifestos. This is something we've discussed a lot in previous interviews. We're living now in a time where there are fewer manifestos. Rem and I made some portraits of the metabolist movement in Japan in which we investigated that moment in the world of architecture when manifestos were still being written. But even then, as the metabolists said in the sixties, there was a kind of irony, or even parody, to the manifestos from the earlier twentieth century. Perhaps you can tell us more about your manifestos and the extent to which they were related to an earlier twentieth-century notion of manifestos.

Gustav Metzger — As a very young student, I eagerly sought out any avant-garde movement and studied it. That must have influenced my later development, when it came to the point when I began to write manifestos.

Hans Ulrich Obrist — What was your first manifesto?

Gustav Metzger — Auto-Destructive Art in the autumn of 1959.

Hans Ulrich Obrist — I'd like to talk a bit about the city. One of the aims of this Marathon is to examine the impossibility of creating a portrait of London. We've heard many different

points of view over the past seventeen, eighteen hours. We were wondering how you see London now, what your perspective on the city is, and how it has changed over the past four or five decades.

Gustav Metzger — Oh, it has changed enormously! I can remember walking once late at night from those big squares near Victoria all the way to Brick Lane, near where I lived. It was just like walking in a village. This was in early 1946, during the winter. There was just the moonlight, and I don't remember seeing any cars [*laughs*]. That's my early experience of London. It was very beautiful—even the bomb sites had a certain beauty. My brother and I worked at the Sir John Cass Institute at Aldgate on a bomb site, carving large bomb site stones. This was in 1946.

Rem Koolhaas — *Many voices from the art world have been represented at this Marathon. Can you comment on your closeness to, or distance from, the artists you've heard today? How does someone like you, who organised an art strike, view the current generation of artists?*

Gustav Metzger — That's difficult. There's so much going on in this country now. Not only in London, but all over the country there's a vast expansion of artistic activity, manifestations, performances, exhibitions—in places that spring up constantly. To judge all of this would be impossible for anybody, certainly for me. But a few general points: I do believe that there's quite a lot of weakness. When I go round the art school diploma exhibitions, I see a lot of weakness, and a lot of playfulness, which does not in the least correspond to the reality of life—neither in this country, nor worldwide. I find this worrying—extremely worrying. Taking the world lightly is just not adequate to this challenge. That's one point of criticism I would make regarding quite a lot of the art—not just among art students and graduates, but generally speaking in exhibitions by younger people.

Hans Ulrich Obrist — Another thing I'd like to discuss is your very unique position in the art world. You've had great influence on several generations of young artists, but you've always remained very independent, especially of the art market. At one point you even called for an art strike. You've put up a lot of resistance to the art world, and have also occasionally disappeared from it. Could you tell us more about your relationship to the world of art?

Gustav Metzger — I think it's necessary to bring in the experiences I had before becoming or trying to become an artist. That was an intense involvement with revolutionary politics, with left-wing socialist/communist ideas and ideals. This took place between the ages of sixteen and eighteen. Then, when I gave up the idea of becoming a political animal, I turned to art. But I maintained my interest in politics, and in revolutionary politics, and I still have that interest. This early excitement influences me constantly. That's the basis of my continuing criticism of art and society. Perhaps I can bring in some points that you haven't asked me about.

Hans Ulrich Obrist — That's a good idea.

Gustav Metzger — I've just made a couple of notes. We're in the middle of a number of paradigm shifts concerning consciousness and the difficulty of going beyond where we are now in understanding our present situation. There's a gap, an enormous gap, between generations, which has exponential aspects. Here, I think, you'll agree. By the way, all I'm talking about is what I read in the media. I'm not a very clever man. I'm responding to and quoting what I read. But let's spend a few minutes on significance. You have the older people, who are not in touch with the actual experience; they can't even get the experience. So the gap is exponential. Every day the young and the very young are moving into it, and the grandparents are not. This is very important and it relates to the earlier point, which is that I believe that the way we—and I mean we in a broad sense—look at reality is so limited compared to the speed of the changes that are happening. Our ways of understanding are simply too slow and too limited. This is one of my great interests. I think it has to do with society, especially those elements of society that desire a change of quality and significance—who need to constantly discuss, and need to understand and communicate. The other point I would like to make is that it's absolutely essential that people act. We have endless talks—and I'm not criticising what we're doing here, as it's good that this event is happening—but there is endless talk among people in the media: 'What shall we do?' I believe that unless some kind of action takes place, it's a waste of time. I'm proposing an action that has to do with the art world. It's to introduce a world campaign with the slogan 'Reduce Art Flights'. The starting point

GOTHENBURG

(CITY)

Discover the best Seafood in the World

FROM £10 ONE WAY

TAXES & CHARGES INCLUDED

RYANAIR.COM

goteborgplus
www.goteborg.com

Book until midnight 07.01.08. Terms & conditions apply. See Ryanair.com for more details. Flights direct from London (Stansted).

would be the next Frieze Art Fair. What I'm saying is, we as a community can't just talk about the problems. We have the opportunity—and, I believe, the absolute responsibility—to act on what we know. We can't go to Beirut and put ourselves physically between the combatants, but we can reduce—not stop, but reduce—flights to art fairs. Just bring it down. That's the campaign, and I hope we achieve some kind of response in the art systems worldwide.

Hans Ulrich Obrist — **It's the third campaign we've had during this Marathon. It started with Eric Hobsbawm saying we should protest against forgetting. Then we had Gilbert & George, who proclaimed a campaign against the rucksack. And now we have a campaign to reduce art flights. I wanted to ask you, in relation to Eric Hobsbawm, whom you appreciate very much, if you could comment on his campaign—on his suggestion that we should have a campaign against forgetting, and on the necessity he sees, with reference to the city, to talk about memory.**

Gustav Metzger — Yes, I'm increasingly concerned with these issues. My last works were in that field. The room at Cubitt Gallery was stating that we must remember the ten thousand and more Jewish intellectuals and artists who were forced to flee and who were destroyed. And the second work, *In Memoriam*, at Basel Kunsthalle early this year was all about recording the memory of the millions of Jews destroyed. This is one direct line I've been working on as an artist over the past year or two, and I will continue in that direction.

Hans Ulrich Obrist — **Many, many thanks Gustav.**

Make air tax greener

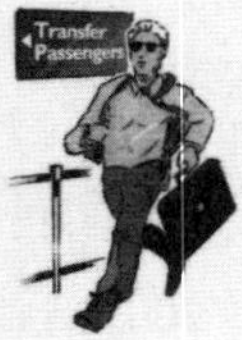

Transfer passengers should pay, just like everyone else

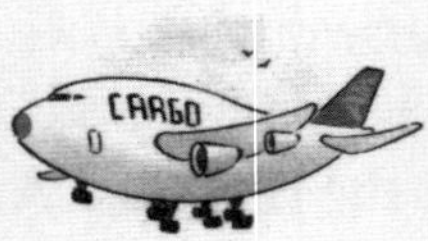

Cargo flights should pay

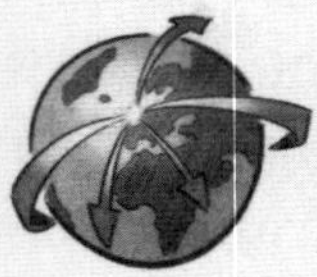

Long haul flights should pay their fair share

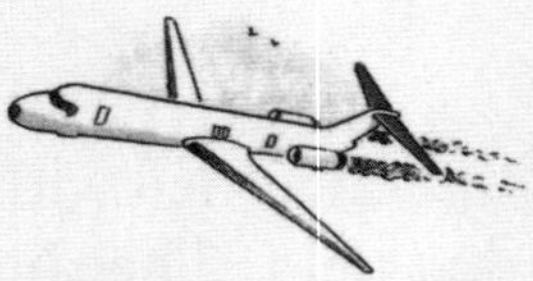

Higher polluting planes should pay more

Air tax is changing. Cut out the subsidies.

easyJet.com

V — Inside / Outside the Art World
Prince's Garden, London, March 31, 2008

Hans Ulrich Obrist — **How has your protest against flying developed since you announced it during the Serpentine Interview Marathon?**

Gustav Metzger — First of all, there was the exhibition in Münster at the Westfälischer Kunstverein ['Gustav Metzger. Models', 2007]. I mentioned the idea of 'Reduce Art Flights' to the Kunstverein Director, Carina Plath and she liked it very much. Between us, we thought we could produce a leaflet. She had 5000 copies done in colour. It looks very good and has now found its way to a large exhibition in Turin on ecology ['Greenwashing. Environment: Perils, Promises and Perplexities', Turin, 2008]. The leaflet there has a different text but is identical in appearance to the one in

Münster. Also, the principle is ongoing and can go anywhere.

Hans Ulrich Obrist — **It's really like a movement now.**

Gustav Metzger — Yes, indeed. And, as you know, it has the colours of the Royal Air Force: red, white, and blue. People are talking about this.

Hans Ulrich Obrist — **Have you founded any other movements lately?**

Gustav Metzger — [*laughs*]

Hans Ulrich Obrist — **You founded the art strike—the art strike was a similar movement.**

Gustav Metzger — You're quite right to remind me. There was a talk about six weeks ago at Beaconsfield [February 6, 2008]; it was the first in a series of three entitled 'Art and Compromise'. They're in a large building, and it was a joint production with City & Guilds of London Art School. The invitation came, and I asked myself what there was to say on the subject. When I started thinking about it, I realised that you can say everything about it—that in art, especially public art, there will be compromise between the commissioner and the artist. In fact, it occurred to me that you could almost call the series 'Art *is* Compromise'. The meeting was absolutely packed out—somehow the word got around, and there were queues round the block. There were all these young people, and I became rather Messianic. Towards the end, I said that we artists can take over the art system, and the galleries can close. The public galleries should continue, and the private galleries can be moved out, can move themselves out of the system. When I speak of artists in this context, I mean art historians, curators, organisers, administrators—the whole machinery. I made similar comments on Saturday during the interview with Andrew Wilson at Tate Modern [March 29, 2008]. Again, I became rather fervent in this direction. I believe this is something that's truly feasible, especially if we consider it in relation to the difficulty of realising a similar idea in 1974, or in the second half of the seventies.

Hans Ulrich Obrist — **When you did the first art strike.**

Gustav Metzger — Yes, when I proposed *Years without Art*—three years without art between 1977 and 1980. But nobody was interested. Nobody. Eventually, Stewart Home took it up ten years later, as you know. The difference between then and now is, I suggest, that we are now far wealthier. Everybody's got a bit of money. Almost everybody. Or they can apply for it, or they can get it from the state. Also, I believe we're becoming more intelligent as a society. I know many people have said that, and I accept the idea. Today you can type in a word on the computer and get a whole page on Lichtenberg or on some obscure philosopher or on me, you, or whoever. You can look up some Greek philosopher whose name has been almost forgotten, and you can start thinking about it and researching it immediately. This just wasn't available a few years ago. At the same time, we're becoming bored with the artist; there's a surfeit of culture and a surfeit of mind, and boredom sets in. We don't like to be bored, so we need something new—something radical. I actually believe that the idea of taking over the art system is something that can be realised in the coming years. We also need to try and phase out the crazy auction houses, where they think they can spiral up the prices endlessly. That should be attacked as part of this movement.

Hans Ulrich Obrist — **From what I've read in your earlier statements, you're basically proposing an economy for artists and art that is different from the economy of the object. Is that correct?**

Gustav Metzger — Exactly.

Hans Ulrich Obrist — **You're also one of the few artists who has resisted this idea of non-objects becoming quasi-objects and thus sellable.**

Gustav Metzger — That's one of the points of auto-destructive art. You can't create an object for sale, unless somebody really wants to exhibit all sorts of art in a gallery. There's nothing to stop them, but I would totally oppose that—it's something I would never do. So the future is bright in the sense that, as you suggested, there are now two movements *im Gang*, underway. I'm happy about this, especially after some years, during which I lived very quietly, and then some years where I concentrated on making exhibitions at the kind invitation of institutions.

Hans Ulrich Obrist — **The exhibition *Life/Live* in Paris was the beginning of your coming back into the world of exhibitions.**

Gustav Metzger — Exactly.

Hans Ulrich Obrist — **I remember very well how reluctant you were.**

Gustav Metzger — After these years of taking part, I now see the need to be the old Metzger, the *aggressive* Metzger [*laughs*].

Hans Ulrich Obrist — **You've often used lectures as your medium. That's also something I wanted to ask you about, because it seems that they're part of your artistic practice.**

Gustav Metzger — Oh, sure, and the lecture/demonstrations.

Hans Ulrich Obrist — **You've been doing a lot of lectures like these again lately—for instance the one you did for us [*Lecture/ Demonstration*, Serpentine Gallery Experiment Marathon, London, 2007].**

Gustav Metzger — That's right.

Hans Ulrich Obrist — **You also did a lecture on Damian [Hirst].**

Gustav Metzger — It's coming back to agitation. Now, of course, I'm very stimulated by the show on the avant-garde at the British Library ['Breaking The Rules: The Printed Face of the European Avant Garde 1900–1937', British Library, London, 2008]. I've spent a lot of time there. There's also the Rodchenko exhibition ['Alexander Rodchenko', Southbank Centre, 2008]. In other words, revolutionary art—radical art—has recently been highlighted in London. This will affect

the aura and the perception in London in relation to radicalism—it must do.

Hans Ulrich Obrist — **This morning I read a very interesting article asking what the chances are for a May 2008.**

Gustav Metzger — Speaking of France, this idea can percolate from country to country. However, I also think it's important to have a fundamental change in the art world—a fundamental change so that artists take over. When I say artists, I'm also thinking of the troops around the artists—the curators, the historians. Art needs this change, and not just because we're getting bored, but because there's a need to introduce seriousness and quality and adventure into art. There's a stepladder at the moment—you start there, and then you go up, and then, if you're very, very lucky, they sell your work at auctions. Then suddenly millions come in. But these stepladders are morally wrong. The other thing is, when you read *The Guardian*, the word ethics predominates. Well, it's not ethical—the art market is not ethical.

Hans Ulrich Obrist — **You say there should be a new radicalism and new manifestos. This general interest in manifestos could also mean that art should be more influential in society. So it's influence more than affluence?**

Gustav Metzger — Exactly, that's part of it. When artists come together in something like cooperatives—we don't even know how it can be done—but when they do, there's already radicalism. Of course, it's not a new idea for artists to exhibit together, but this could be more or less institutionalised: when they leave art school, artists could go into some place where they can exhibit their work and offer it for sale, rather than through the galleries. In the next few years, the challenge will be to solidify these different ideas into proposals, into writing, and to circulate them and stimulate the young people, especially, to act within the framework of these ideas. And again, when talking at Beaconsfield, I could sense that the young people in the audience were perceptive and were waiting for some kind of lead.

Hans Ulrich Obrist — **What would your advice be to young artists in 2008?**

Gustav Metzger — To young artists?

Hans Ulrich Obrist — **Rainer Maria Rilke wrote this lovely advice to a young poet, so I was wondering what your advice to a young artist would be.**[21]

Gustav Metzger — Well, first of all, I'd recommend seeing the exhibition of avant-garde material at the British Library. The exhibition has ended, but all the material is at the British Library.

Hans Ulrich Obrist — **Is there a catalogue?**

Gustav Metzger — There is a catalogue, but of course it's not comprehensive.[22] The show was enormous. All the

(21) Rainer Maria Rilke, *Briefe an einen jungen Dichter* (Leipzig: Insel, 1929). Engl.: *Letters to a young poet* (Mineola, N.Y.: Dover Publications, 2002).
(22) Stephen Bury (ed.), *Breaking the Rules. The Printed Face of the European Avant Garde 1900–1937* (London: British Library, 2007).

material is there, however, so you can always get a day-ticket, or you become a member of the British Library.

Hans Ulrich Obrist — **That's your first piece of advice.**

Gustav Metzger — Yes, and then I would advise them to go back to Russian constructivism. In fact, I would advise young people to go back to Russia from 1900 onwards, which would then include socialist realism. It's very important to see all that, to take it in—it's all very fascinating. There's an enormous amount of literature on the subject.

Hans Ulrich Obrist — **That would be the second piece of advice.**

Gustav Metzger — Yes, and then I would recommend that they think about building cooperatives, with the aim of moving out of the commercial art galleries. When that happens, the volume of advertisements in the art magazines will shrink, which I think is important. Again, one of the reasons I'm attacking the art world is because of the bloated nature of the leading art magazines, which are, to a large extent, advertisements.

Hans Ulrich Obrist — **So today, after your protest against all the flying taking place between art fairs, you're protesting against advertising.**

Gustav Metzger — The advertisements in the magazines take up most of the space, and they inevitably involve compromise. There is a compromise between the intentions of the artist and the demands of commerce. So you see, these magazines are monuments to compromise. That's what should be questioned, criticised, and reduced. With mobile telephones and e-mail, an idea can spread like a virus—an idea *is* a virus. It can spread within seconds. So this can be to the advantage of the idea.

Hans Ulrich Obrist — To conclude I'd like to ask you one more question about your use of lectures as a medium. Your lecture about Damien Hirst and his skull was a lecture or talk. However, you also do talks that involve experiments, like the one you did for the Marathon. Can you explain the difference between the experiment talks and the lectures?

Gustav Metzger — The lecture/demonstration of auto-destructive art began with the event at the Temple Gallery in London in June 1960. As time went by, I gave several more lecture/demonstrations of auto-destructive art. They eventually came to an end, and just became talks without demonstrations. So that's the state I'm in now—the state of talking, rather than talking and demonstrating.

Hans Ulrich Obrist — So what you did for the Serpentine Experiment Marathon was to revisit one of your earlier lecture/demonstrations.

Gustav Metzger — That's right. I was re-creating a part of the first lecture/demonstration.

Hans Ulrich Obrist — With the metal?

Gustav Metzger — With the metal, yes. That's what it was, a reconstruction. In other words, I showed, at your invitation, a segment of the big table, which, by the way, is now in the Tate collection, including the metal rods that were made over a period of three weeks by a young lady. It was a very, very difficult task.

Hans Ulrich Obrist — **So it's a big table with several demonstrations?**

Gustav Metzger — Yes, with several objects on it and the remnant of an *Acid Nylon* painting as a background.

Hans Ulrich Obrist — **There are so many lectures.**

Gustav Metzger — I actually haven't done many, but you can go to the Tate Archive. They have manuscripts of some of the talks I've given since 1996.

Hans Ulrich Obrist — **Is there any lecture in particular you'd like to mention—one you feel is particularly significant?**

Gustav Metzger — Well, in the Tate Archive they have, to my knowledge, *Mad Cows Talk* [East West Gallery, London, 1996], which went over to Paris. So this lecture is important for me.

Hans Ulrich Obrist — **That was shown at the Musée d'Art moderne de la Ville de Paris.**

Gustav Metzger — That's right, at the *Life/Live* exhibition. So that's one I would mention in particular.

Hans Ulrich Obrist — **Often your lectures are very encyclopaedic, developed out of newspapers. It was a mad cow iconography.**

Gustav Metzger — Unfortunately, the slides are gone.

JANUARY SALE

2 MILLION SEATS

FROM £10

ONE WAY, TAXES & CHARGES INCLUDED

TRAVEL MONDAY - SUNDAY

WWW.RYANAIR.COM

RYANAIR GIFT VOUCHERS FROM £20

Book until midnight tonight. Subject to availability, terms & conditions. Flights direct from London (Stansted).

Hans Ulrich Obrist — **They've been lost?**

Gustav Metzger — They've got some of them left, but the order—it's not available. But regarding the talk, the interview on Saturday at Tate Modern with Andrew Wilson, we started by showing an eleven-minute film of the Sharjah Biennale installation taken from a helicopter. Very beautiful. You probably haven't seen it.

Hans Ulrich Obrist — **No, I haven't.**

Gustav Metzger — The project with 120 cars pumping their exhaust into the structure covered by polythene was finally realised there. This film shows that work.

Hans Ulrich Obrist — **So it's finally been realised!**

Gustav Metzger — Yes, it has. On Saturday we showed an eleven-minute film, shot from a helicopter, of the large project and then a projection of eleven or twelve colour illustrations taken from newspapers. So you see, this is still ongoing for me—the connection with the daily images we have, and presenting it to an art public. There is continuity. Colour photographs were made, and we showed them. So people got the feel of contact with the present day, which is so important to me.

Hans Ulrich Obrist — **That's why newspapers play such a big role in your work, isn't it? The newspapers bring that in.**

Gustav Metzger — It's the present day. It's this concern of mine with changing, with decanting the art system. It's not a question of destroying it. We don't want to get rid of it, to stand and throw bricks. We want to decant it—take out its energy, the money that's involved, and then start again.

Hans Ulrich Obrist — **Now that your Sharjah piece has been realised, do you still have unrealised projects?**

Gustav Metzger — I do, in fact. In Sharjah the motors were running for one week. Ideally, though, they should have run for the whole duration of the Biennale. That wasn't possible, and it also wasn't exactly 120 cars—it was 100, for different reasons. So in fact the original project hasn't been realised. But this Sharjah piece is just phase one; phase two is when the cars are destroyed, when they destroy themselves. That's still waiting to be realised.

Hans Ulrich Obrist — **Thank you so much, Gustav.**

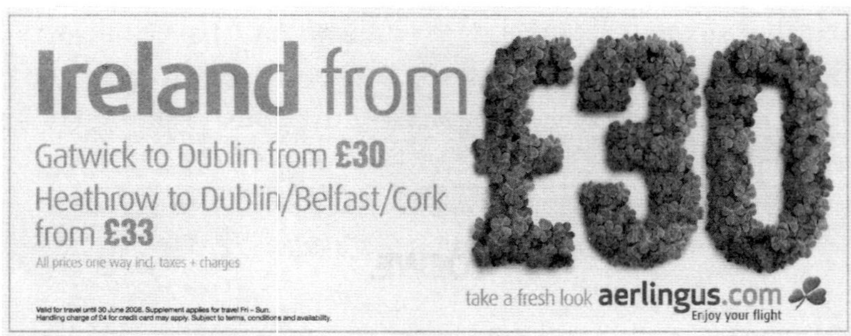
Ireland from £30
Gatwick to Dublin from £30
Heathrow to Dublin/Belfast/Cork from £33
All prices one way incl. taxes + charges
Valid for travel until 30 June 2008. Supplement applies for travel Fri – Sun.
Handling charge of £4 for credit card may apply. Subject to terms, conditions and availability.
take a fresh look aerlingus.com
Enjoy your flight

VI — Missing Links
Serpentine Gallery, June 2008

Hans Ulrich Obrist — We recently spoke about your beginnings, and it was all connected to Lord [Arnold] Goodman. I know Lord Goodman was a very influential man in England from the sixties onwards, but I didn't realise that there was this relationship with art and with you.

Gustav Metzger — The contact started through a solicitor's office, an established firm run by Mr. Royalton-Kisch, and Arnold Goodman was a young man who acted as one of his assistants. My brother and I had been recommended for a grant by our teacher David Bomberg. In the course of getting that grant, we were introduced to the solicitor's office. Mr. Royalton-Kisch and Arnold Goodman were in charge of administering the grant for the next two years.

Hans Ulrich Obrist — **This was in the fifties?**

Gustav Metzger — The contact started in the early spring of 1946, and went on for two years.

Hans Ulrich Obrist — **So Lord Goodman was a young man at the time.**

Gustav Metzger — At that time he was a young man. Both my brother and I went to the Continent in the summer of 1948, and we studied in academies in Antwerp and Brussels for a year. I came back at the end of '49. My studies in Antwerp began in the autumn of '48 and ended in the summer of '49. I travelled again in France and then returned to England. At that point, the question was if my grant would be renewed, and in the context of that renewal, Arnold Goodman, who was still in the same office, offered to take drawings of mine, which I had done on the Continent, for approval or otherwise, to Jacob Epstein. A dinner was arranged where Arnold Goodman showed Epstein my drawings made in Antwerp, and Epstein was very supportive in getting another grant. Apparently he liked the drawings very much. Now, talking of Goodman, the very interesting thing is that, at that meeting, he was introduced to people in the music sphere, the music business. Within a short period of time, Goodman became very active as an agent for people in music. To some extent, this was a turning point in his career, taking these drawings, making contact with one of the great British artists.

Hans Ulrich Obrist — **So he mainly put young artists in touch with Jacob Epstein.**

Gustav Metzger — He got in touch with musicians and the music sphere and built up connections as an adviser, a solicitor for people in music. From there, he went into other arts, and so for him this meeting with Epstein was a kind of introduction to the world of art, which he specialised in for the rest of his life.

Hans Ulrich Obrist — **We haven't spoken about Epstein. Was he important for you?**

Gustav Metzger — Yes. I admired a great deal of his work. I saw lots of it. He exhibited repeatedly in London. For example, at Temple Newsam near Leeds, where I first came across modern art, there was an exhibition of Epstein in conjunction with Matthew Smith ['Jacob Epstein, Matthew Smith', Temple Newsam House, 1942]. In London, the two large works in St James, the headquarters of London Underground, had a tremendous impact on me when I saw them as a young man in '45 or '46.

Hans Ulrich Obrist — **And Lord Goodman became a long-term support to you.**

Gustav Metzger — Yes, that's a fact. In the seventies I had difficulties in managing my life, and he offered to give me a personal grant for several years, which was very important for me in terms of survival. On and off I would visit him to ask his advice—what I should do next, or whether I should take a lease on some rooms. As you know, there was a problem with the [Hermann] Nitsch event [5th Abreaktionsspiel of OM Theatre, DIAS, September, 1966], where the police came and

DANGER!
FALLING PRICES

	WAS	NOW
BELFAST (CITY AIRPORT)	~~£10~~	£5
BRUSSELS (CHARLEROI)	~~£10~~	£5
DERRY	~~£10~~	£5
GDANSK	~~£10~~	£5
GLASGOW (PRETWICK)	~~£10~~	£5
KLAGENFURT	~~£10~~	£5
PALMA MALLORA	~~£10~~	£5
REUS (BARCELONA)	~~£10~~	£5
SHANNON	~~£10~~	£5
TOULON	~~£10~~	£5

ONE WAY FROM, INCLUDES ALL TAXES & CHARGES

WWW.**RYANAIR**.COM

AVIONIC MECHANIC VACANCIES APPLY ON WWW.RYANAIR.COM

Book until midnight tonight. Subject to availability, terms & conditions. Flights direct from London (Stansted).

we, John Sharkey and I, were charged with putting on the performance. While this was going on, I went to see Lord Goodman, who was Chairman of the Arts Council at the time. I made an appointment to see him at his office, and he became quite aggressive and said, 'This shouldn't have happened.' I was very shocked, and, of course, hurt. I had a feeling that he somehow had to defend some position. I'm not sure at all that he actually had this aggressive stance towards Nitsch. I'm not sure if this was his real feeling.

Hans Ulrich Obrist — **Did you reconcile with him later?**

Gustav Metzger — It did cool the relationship between us, and for me it certainly was a crucial experience. He was actually quite gentle, very quiet, when I first met him. But eventually he got very big, physically, and very powerful and very short of time. Everybody wanted to consult him. But for me it was an important contact, of course, essentially very helpful. He helped me a great deal.

Hans Ulrich Obrist — **And he brought up Epstein. What was your direct interaction with Epstein? You said you met him indirectly.**

Gustav Metzger — I met Moore.

Hans Ulrich Obrist — **You never met Epstein personally?**

Gustav Metzger — Epstein had annual exhibitions at the Leicester Galleries, which were on Leicester Square then. Bomberg encouraged the students to go there. We could get in for free; we said that we were students of Bomberg and we didn't have to pay. I often saw this man, and I knew who he was. He always had this huge cloak on—a very large figure, a very powerful impression, but I never ever talked to him. There was this indirect contact, however, through Goodman and the drawings. I did like a lot of his work. I still do. At the moment there are some of his works in the sculpture gallery at the V&A. Very powerful. He had a very hard life, as you know. He came here as a totally poor person. He was struggling to get established. A lot of people didn't like him because he was so original, so distinctive, and Jewish on top of all that. There's also the tragedy of his sculptures at Rhodesia House in the Strand, which were beginning to crumble and were fenced in with metal mesh so they wouldn't collapse. They were eventually defaced. We lost about a dozen of his major sculptures.

Hans Ulrich Obrist — **You said you were making drawings at the time, and even before you came to England?**

Gustav Metzger — No, before I came to England I was twelve.

Hans Ulrich Obrist — **So you started when you were in England.**

Gustav Metzger — Yes. The exact date is 1945.

Hans Ulrich Obrist — **What would be the earliest preserved work?**

Gustav Metzger — There could be a few drawings somewhere in a box. I kept drawings. There could be a few drawings from Cambridge School of Art.

Hans Ulrich Obrist — **Were they abstract?**

Gustav Metzger — No, they were from life and weren't very good, because I was just beginning in Cambridge. In January '45 I was just starting.

Hans Ulrich Obrist — **When I saw your piece in the 'Out of Actions' exhibition in Los Angeles, that's really the step that went far beyond abstract expressionism ['Out of Actions. Between Performance and the Object 1949–1979', MOCA, Los Angeles, 1998].**

Gustav Metzger — You mean the *Acid Nylon*?

Hans Ulrich Obrist — **Yes, that went beyond anything that had happened in painting before. What was the trajectory from the early figurative drawings to these very radical works? Was it a gradual development, or was there a sudden breakthrough?**

Gustav Metzger — It certainly has to do with the teachings of David Bomberg, who encouraged the artists—in this case the students—to use their body, to interact physically. This relates to abstract expressionism, to the American developments going on at the same time, in 1945–46, when I entered the class. It goes back to the period when I was introduced to drawing that was completely different to what I had been doing in Cambridge, which had involved following the outline of the figure, to make a realistic interpretation. Bomberg said, 'Forget about that! Go for the structure! Go for the centre, and use the full weight of your body!' That was the beginning of my move towards the end result, towards dealing with the central, salient points of the figure, rather than with the detail—going to the heart of the matter. That's Bomberg. As you know, I stayed with Bomberg from 1945 till 1953, with some interruptions. It was a very long time, eight years of contact with Bomberg—a productive contact.

Hans Ulrich Obrist — **Where would your catalogue raisonné begin? If we were to sketch a catalogue of your œuvre, what would be the first work you stand behind?**

Gustav Metzger — It would be some of the work I did with Bomberg in his class. For example, there were days, or rather evenings, when the model didn't turn up, so Bomberg would say, 'Would you come and be the model for tonight?' It was unpaid, of course. Auerbach was the model several times. I have paintings, portraits of Auerbach, which would be included, partly because Auerbach is now a world concept, a world image. So I would start with those. And I would start with other paintings done in 1946 in Bomberg's composition class, which took place in a period of time in '46, alongside the evening class. Then we could go to the period in King's Lynn. The classes stopped in '53. Between '53 and '56 I didn't paint at all. But in '56 I was living in a wonderful, huge house, all by myself, and one room was set up as a studio, where I began to paint seriously. I would also include some of the paintings from '56 to '59, when I moved to London. They're abstract. They're not figurative, although there was a small series of tables I did during that period.

Hans Ulrich Obrist — **Table sculptures?**

Gustav Metzger — No. I had a circular wooden table in my studio, and I would paint that as a subject. The biggest painting of the table was the best, and it was very violent. In fact, it looked a bit like an explosion. It was in browns and black—very strong. I think that would be included, too, if only because it's the first one where the atom bomb came in. But then, speaking of that, in Antwerp I did at least one painting of the town and the Schelde—the river in front. So towards the end of my stay, which started in the autumn of '48 and ended in the summer, towards the end of that first half year, I did some drawings of Antwerp from the other side of the river. I did at least one painting where you saw the town, which I entitled *Antwerp After a Nuclear Attack*.

Hans Ulrich Obrist — **Perhaps that was the beginning of the autodestructive moment.**

Gustav Metzger — Yes, the interest in destruction, in an art context. That would be a definite bridge—Antwerp, summer of '49. It was a very warm summer, and I would spend hours and hours in the street drawing children who just went by, and I would say, 'Stand still for ten minutes.' They were all very, very sad—all almost crying. These are the drawings I gave to Goodman to show to Epstein. Very emotional images.

Hans Ulrich Obrist — **That leads back to the beginning of our conversation. This is where Goodman started, where he came in.**

Gustav Metzger — That's how Goodman continued supporting me. This would have been in 1950.

Hans Ulrich Obrist — **And after that? What was the next cycle?**

Gustav Metzger — Then we have this period in King's Lynn with the explosive table, which, by the way, was bought by a friend of mine, who then moved to the Caribbean, and I'm hoping to trace him one day. So one of the few works I ever sold was to this friend, who was also a member of the Committee of 100. That's the other connection, which started in late 1960, where I was an active member. Then there's a real turning point in King's Lynn. I was painting on boards, essentially, rather than canvas, with a palette knife for two or three years, but it wasn't hard enough. So I realised I must buy some metal. I bought three sheets of metal, quite big, and they looked grey, of course. Then I took my palette knife and painted. While painting I would inevitably incise the metal. For the first time, I had a kinetic element in my art, and kinetics became so important.

Hans Ulrich Obrist — **Do these pieces still exist?**

Gustav Metzger — Yes, they do.

Hans Ulrich Obrist — **So they're like metallic paintings of some sort.**

Gustav Metzger — Yes, the metal comes through—especially in one of them. And then something else happened.

Hans Ulrich Obrist — **Was that in 1960?**

Gustav Metzger — '59, or actually '58. The turning of the two years. What happened: on one of these paintings, the best of them, I picked up a piece of chalk and made some marks. That was something I'd never done before. In the literature by Andrew Wilson, there's a specific reference to that. Also, this work is reproduced in the book by Stephen Bann called *Experimental Painting*.[23] Bann speaks about this. It was less than a year before my first manifesto on auto-destructive art. So these chalk marks on the painting, and the painting itself, are a turning point. I think that's the real turning point from painting to acid and nylon.

Hans Ulrich Obrist — **And then, soon afterwards, came the cardboard exhibition.**

Gustav Metzger — That's right. A year later, in London, I was totally unprepared, but, I want to emphasise, I had been looking for something new all the time, from the beginning of my studies with Bomberg or even before, and especially when I came to London, the avant-garde, the next step, is what really was important to me. The next step in art, and my next step. And this is still the case: I want to paint for the next step, for something beyond at least my present capacities. That's what concerns me.

Hans Ulrich Obrist — **Thank you very much.**

(23) Stephen Bann, *Experimental Painting, Construction, Abstraction, Destruction, Reduction* (New York: Universe, 1970).

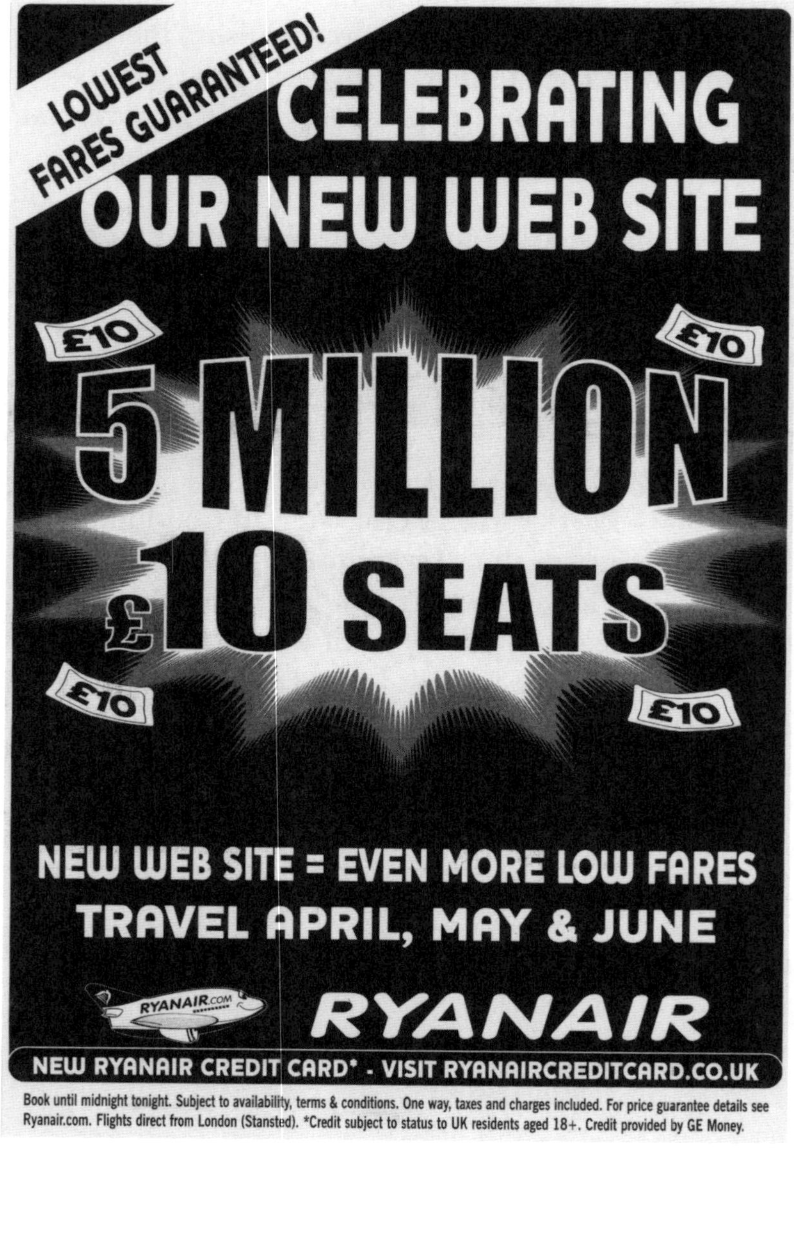

LOWEST FARES GUARANTEED!
CELEBRATING OUR NEW WEB SITE
£10
£10
5 MILLION
£10 SEATS
£10
£10
NEW WEB SITE = EVEN MORE LOW FARES
TRAVEL APRIL, MAY & JUNE
RYANAIR.COM
RYANAIR
NEW RYANAIR CREDIT CARD* - VISIT RYANAIRCREDITCARD.CO.UK
Book until midnight tonight. Subject to availability, terms & conditions. One way, taxes and charges included. For price guarantee details see Ryanair.com. Flights direct from London (Stansted). *Credit subject to status to UK residents aged 18+. Credit provided by GE Money.

VII — Berlin Interview Marathon
Buchhandlung Walther König an der Museumsinsel
July 6, 2008

Hans Ulrich Obrist — Please give a warm welcome to our next guest, Gustav Metzger. I'd like to start by discussing a specific protest Kasper König reminded me about. Gustav, you, Klaus Staeck, and Cordula Frowein staged a powerful protest at the 'Westkunst' exhibition in Cologne in 1981. Could you tell us something about that?

Gustav Metzger — I'd rather not, because I was hoping to talk more about the present than the past. That was very, very long ago. At the moment I'd rather focus on how we are now.

Hans Ulrich Obrist — Fair enough. I should mention to our audience that we first met in the mid-nineties. Back then, after a long absence from the art world—after your famous art strike—you returned with a small exhibition in a bookshop, in which discursive events and exhibitions also took place. The place was called *workfortheeyetodo*. Your *Historic Photographs* were exhibited for the first time in this book space in London, too. A book was also published with your texts as part of the project.[24] That was shortly before *Life/Live*, our first cooperation, where you made a large installation at the Musée d'Art moderne in Paris. Twelve years have passed since then, and you've taken part in exhibitions consistently, the last one being the skulptur projekte in Münster. And last, but not least, we've had many conversations over the years; it all began in Café Cosmo at Waterloo in London. In your most recent talks, you've suggested a number of times that you're planning on leaving the art world again, and you've started some new protests. Perhaps we could start with these.

Gustav Metzger — Yes, I'd rather start with these.

Hans Ulrich Obrist — The first protest is something you talked about during our Serpentine Marathon with Rem Koolhaas—it was the protest against all the flying taking place between art fairs and exhibitions. It's a protest that has emerged at several exhibitions, most recently at Rebaudengo in Turin. Can you tell me how this new protest came about?

Gustav Metzger — On the weekend when Art Basel opened in June 2006, I suddenly had the idea that I should protest against the endless flying in the art world—of artworks, of curators, of collectors, all from one part of the world to another. Then I came up with the slogan 'Reduce Art Flights', and when you write it down, it's RAF, as in the Royal Air Force, the military part of

(24) Gustav Metzger, *damaged nature, auto-destructive art* (London: coracle@workfortheeyetodo, 1996).

flying in England. That was, of course, an important term in the war, the Second World War—a terribly important symbol, an image: RAF. So I called some friends in Basel. I couldn't go there, and I asked if they could do something. It was too difficult, though, because there wasn't enough time to organise anything, but I thought about it continuously. After I mentioned it briefly at the Marathon, however, the idea went online in *Artforum* and all round the world.

Hans Ulrich Obrist — **Then it came to Münster, right?**

Gustav Metzger — Yes. In Münster we talked about it, and the Director of the Kunstverein, Carina Plath, made the decision to turn this theme, this RAF, into a leaflet. Together with the Kunstverein Münster, we made an edition of 5000 sheets. These were displayed at the Kunstverein, and then a group of young artists living in Barcelona were planning an exhibition in Turin. They wanted to adopt the idea, and on the basis of the leaflet from Münster they created a leaflet in Italian for Turin. If people want it, it can go round the world bit by bit. I'm still very much hoping that this minimal campaign in the art world will be pushed through against processes that are so harmful and dangerous.

Hans Ulrich Obrist — **When we first met, you were busy with an archive that became a great work: *Mad Cows Talk*—an encyclopaedia of English newspaper clippings about this topic, and that became a slideshow.**

Gustav Metzger — Fifty slides.

Hans Ulrich Obrist — **Now, parallel to your protest against flying, you've begun to compile a similar archive of all those ads from low-budget airlines.**

Gustav Metzger — Most of the ads are from Ryanair, which is the cheapest of the cheap airlines in Great Britain. They're placed systematically in various newspapers.

Hans Ulrich Obrist — **You came up with the idea of using them as illustrations for our conversation book.**

Gustav Metzger — Yes, thirty pieces, thirty illustrations.

Hans Ulrich Obrist — **Will the archive continue to grow?**

Gustav Metzger — I suppose when our book is published, that will be about the end of it.

Hans Ulrich Obrist — **You've always said that newspapers play an important role for you. In your studio, you have a large archive with piles and piles of newspapers. Tell us something about your archive and how it functions.**

Gustav Metzger — The answer is that it doesn't function at all, because everything is on top of everything else; there's no system whatsoever. To find the things we needed for our book, it took me days of ransacking. I don't see it as a problem as long as I can keep it all. But after so many years, it has to stop someday; it's becoming too much. The collection gets too big, and you have to give it up at a certain point—when you move, for example.

Hans Ulrich Obrist — **You told me in one of our conversations that newspapers are important for you, and I quote: 'This is still ongoing for me—the connection with the daily images we have, and presenting it to an art public. There is a continuity. It wasn't planned by me; it just happened.' You've also spoken about the contact with the present day that can be established through newspapers. This is related to the airline ads now, but also to a work you did for the Serpentine in London about Damien Hirst's skull, where you established different archives of newspapers. That became a lecture, too. Perhaps we can talk about the new lectures you've given over the past two years.**

Gustav Metzger — For me, lectures are the possibility to express what I'm engaged in at the moment. Of course, that changes with time, and with the times. My contact with society is restricted, so the lectures are a possibility to communicate with people in a direct way. What I emphasise in my lectures is the necessity for art to deal with important issues and directions in society. And in the centre of what's important to me, there's a word beginning with c, and that's capitalism. So constantly making connections between what's happening and the principles of capitalism—that's what is most significant in these lectures.

Hans Ulrich Obrist — **Could you describe your Damien Hirst lecture? It was about Damien's skull and the way the press in England reviewed it.**

Gustav Metzger — I received your invitation to a conference in an important place—in Conway Hall in Holborn, in the centre of London. For many, many decades, maybe back to the First World War, it's been a place

Think Flybe...Think Local

Flight Sale Now On!

fly from £21.99 one way

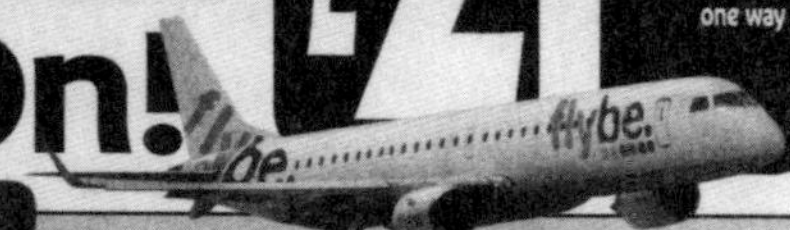

UK REGIONS

Route	fares from
BIRMINGHAM TO:	
NEW Dundee*	£53.70
Aberdeen	£24.99
Inverness	£49.99
Belfast City	£34.99
Newquay	£43.99
Glasgow	£24.99
Edinburgh	£24.99
Isle of Man	£29.99
CARDIFF TO:	
Belfast City	£24.99
Edinburgh	£24.99
Glasgow	£24.99
Jersey	£44.99
Newcastle	£31.99
MANCHESTER TO:	
Glasgow	£27.99
Inverness	£27.99
Edinburgh	£27.99
Guernsey	£45.99
Jersey	£56.99
Belfast City	£22.99
Exeter	£29.99
GUERNSEY TO:	
Birmingham	£54.99
Exeter	£31.99
Southampton	£34.99
NEWCASTLE TO:	
Belfast City	£21.99
Exeter	£27.99
Southampton	£29.99
JERSEY TO:	
Edinburgh	£63.99
Southampton	£31.99
Birmingham	£59.99
Exeter	£31.99
Newcastle	£34.99
Doncaster Sheffield	£59.99
London Southend	£64.99
NORWICH TO:	
Jersey	£64.99
Manchester	£29.99
Edinburgh	£29.99
SOUTHAMPTON TO:	
Isle of Man	£51.99
Inverness	£66.99
Manchester	£29.99
Glasgow	£55.99
Edinburgh	£52.99
Aberdeen	£51.99
Belfast City	£39.99
LONDON GATWICK TO:	
Newcastle	£44.99
Belfast City	£24.99
Aberdeen	£44.99
Inverness	£31.99
Isle of Man	£54.99
Jersey	£29.99
Guernsey	£31.99
BELFAST CITY TO:	
NEW Dundee*	£49.00
Inverness	£31.99
Doncaster Sheffield	£24.99
Exeter	£29.99
Glasgow	£22.99
Edinburgh	£22.99
Aberdeen	£31.99
GLASGOW TO:	
Jersey	£68.99
BRISTOL TO:	
Jersey	£32.99
EDINBURGH TO:	
Newquay	£31.99
EXETER TO:	
Inverness	£64.99
Glasgow	£56.99
Edinburgh	£55.99
ISLE OF MAN TO:	
NEW Newquay	£34.99
London Luton	£49.99
Liverpool	£21.99
Manchester	£21.99
LEEDS BRADFORD TO:	
Belfast City	£24.99
Exeter	£27.99
Southampton	£29.99

EUROPEAN CITIES

Route	fares from
BIRMINGHAM TO:	
Hamburg	£37.99
Dusseldorf	£37.99
Frankfurt	£39.99
Milan	£39.99
Stuttgart	£39.99
Hannover	£54.99
Paris	£39.99
MANCHESTER TO:	
Brussels	£69.99
Dusseldorf	£67.99
Frankfurt	£34.99
Hannover	£61.99
Milan	£39.99
Paris	£64.99
SOUTHAMPTON TO:	
Frankfurt	£34.99
Amsterdam	£53.99
Dusseldorf	£34.99
Hannover	£51.99
Paris	£59.99
Brussels	£39.99
SOUTHAMPTON TO:	
Dublin	£27.99
Alicante	£59.99
Palma	£49.99
GUERNSEY TO:	
NEW Dublin	£39.99
NEW Paris	£39.99
BELFAST CITY TO:	
Paris	£65.99
NORWICH TO:	
Paris	£34.99
Dublin	£29.99
CARDIFF TO:	
Paris	£34.99
EXETER TO:	
Amsterdam	£29.99
Brussels	£34.99
Paris	£44.99
Dublin	£55.99
Palma	£49.99
JERSEY TO:	
NEW Paris	£39.99

REGIONAL FRANCE

Route	fares from
BIRMINGHAM TO:	
Paris	£39.99
Brest Brittany	£51.99
BELFAST CITY TO:	
Paris	£65.99
Rennes	£54.99
MANCHESTER TO:	
Paris	£64.99
Brest Brittany	£64.99
Rennes	£65.99
La Rochelle	£54.99
NORWICH TO:	
Paris	£34.99
CARDIFF TO:	
Paris	£34.99
NEWCASTLE TO:	
Rennes	£39.99
GUERNSEY TO:	
NEW Paris	£39.99
EDINBURGH TO:	
Rennes	£70.99
SOUTHAMPTON TO:	
Paris	£59.99
Rennes	£49.99
Brest Brittany	£31.99
Avignon	£59.99
La Rochelle	£54.99
Perpignan	£59.99
JERSEY TO:	
NEW Paris	£39.99
GLASGOW TO:	
Paris	£59.99
La Rochelle	£59.99
LONDON GATWICK TO:	
Bergerac	£54.99
EXETER TO:	
Paris	£44.99
Rennes	£49.99
Nice	£54.99
Bergerac	£54.99
Avignon	£54.99

GREAT REASONS TO CHOOSE FLYBE FOR TRAVEL

- Have a lie in and check-in online from home
- Rewards4all - fly 4 times get 1 free
- Flybe Economy Plus - the only low cost airline to offer a business service
- Sit together - pre-assign your seat in advance
- Work needn't stop at the airport with Flybe executive lounges across the UK & Europe
- Get back to put the kids to bed with high frequency schedules - up to 8 flights a day

SPECIAL OFFERS!

	fares from		fares from
Edinburgh	£22.99	Milan	£39.99
Belfast City	£21.99	Dublin	£27.99
Manchester	£21.99	Paris	£39.99
Frankfurt	£34.99	Bergerac	£54.99
	all fares are one way		all fares are one way

flybe.com

Europe's local airline.

Fares are one way including taxes & charges, only available online, subject to availability. £2.99 handling fee applies to all credit cards & £1.10 for debit cards per passenger per one way flight, minimum fee may apply. 21 day advance purchase required. Available for travel on or before 25.10.08. Not all routes operate throughout the entire travel period, see website for details. Book by 30.06.08. Fly 4 times get 1 free is based on Flybe Economy Plus travel.

where left-wing people and radical societies and associations gathered and talked about their ideas. For example, in Conway Hall the *Destruction in Art Symposium* took place on several evenings, with demonstrations by the Viennese Actionists. I spent weeks trying to find illustrations of the skull, not only at home but in libraries. That was a very interesting time for me, very exciting, and the illustrations are fascinating indeed. I got direct access to the skull through the Serpentine Gallery and was able to make a very short inspection. To my surprise I found it to be a very beautiful, exciting experience. I thought it was really strong and very moving. It's fairly small—no bigger than this hand. As you know, during the lecture I attacked the art system very intensively.

Hans Ulrich Obrist — **This leads us to the meeting on 'Art and Compromise' at Beaconsfield in February. You said, and I quote: 'There were all these young people, and I became rather Messianic. Towards the end, I said that we artists can take over the art system, and the galleries can close. The public galleries should continue, and the private galleries can be moved out, can move themselves out of the system.' Can you tell us more about this?**

Gustav Metzger — Oh, yes, I'd like to, because I see the situation in the art world as separated from the world as it is. I see the possibility, and the *necessity*, to do a minimum. A minimum, for example, is 'Reduce Art Flights'. I see the possibility that artists will increasingly take over their own lives, their own production, in relation to society in a wider sense, instead of trying to enter existing galleries. I see the possibility of us bringing our work to the public by ourselves, in big halls, in houses, where more people, more artists can exhibit than would be possible in private galleries. That's part of the attack on capitalism. I've argued in that direction in various lectures in recent times. By having more money, on average, than twenty years ago, and with computers, the internet, and mobile phones, we have the ability to take over the power that lies partly in the hands of the private galleries. I think this is a necessary step. How do you do that? Piece by piece we take the energy and money and power out of the existing systems, and we transfer this money and the power and these possibilities in a cooperative manner. This can happen globally. As I see it, now is the time, now it is possible because of the circumstances. And another thing: through the internet and other means of modern communication, people have the possibility to become more intelligent, to learn more, to put things into effect more actively and more quickly. If we keep that in mind and, even more importantly, when we see how radically the world has changed in the last twenty years and how the world will radicalise more and more, I see a concept that can pervade the art world: we need to radicalise, otherwise we will lose contact to this constantly radicalising and increasingly dangerous world. We mustn't remain in a kind of ghetto, on an island of art, where we deal only with art, with art organisers, with money and power. We are marginalised by a world that is totally different, that is extremely brutal, and that deals with tremendous power and enormous financial means. This implies the disintegration of art and the disintegration of the artist.

That's how I see it. *We cannot radicalise enough against a radicalising world.*

Hans Ulrich Obrist — **In our conversation in London not long ago, you referred to your background in revolutionary politics. Could you tell us more about this?**

Gustav Metzger — It mainly has to do with Germany. One of the earliest memories is from my childhood in Nuremberg. We were living in a house in Fürther Straße, which is a big, linear road from Nuremberg to Fürth. We were at the beginning of that road, Fürther Straße 37. We had a big yard in front of our home. One day I went into the yard and onto the road and joined a marching group of political people. I think they were more left-wing than right-wing. This was before '33. It was, I believe, my first appearance in politics. But my parents were very worried and took me back home as quickly as possible, and I was locked up, grounded for some days. During the war I was in England—in Leeds, an industrial city, where I studied cabinet making and worked in a furniture factory. There I met a young man who was a keen Trotskyite, and he introduced me to left-wing politics. That was very exciting. He gave me literature about what was to become the Militant Tendency, a Trotskyite organisation. Then I read Lenin for about two years, and some Marx, and I became something of a communist. In the spring of '44, I went to Bristol to live in a commune of Trotskyites and anarchists. But after six months I decided I'd rather be an artist than a politician, so I started my studies as an artist in January 1945. My interest in politics didn't just stop; without a doubt it continued, through my studies, until now.

Hans Ulrich Obrist — **So you moved from your work with wood to the world of art. Did you go to Bomberg immediately? How did that happen? You also met Paolozzi very early, as a student.**

Gustav Metzger — Yes, that's right. There was an encounter with Paolozzi at the Ashmolean Museum, where I thought I might study, at the Slade School of Art, which had been evacuated to Oxford during the war. When I went to see if I could study there, I met this young man—Paolozzi. We talked for five minutes. He didn't know who I was, and I didn't know who he was. We were both young people. He told me straightforwardly, 'This is a terrible school. You shouldn't come here.' So I decided that if a student thought that, and I wasn't really interested in going there anyway, then I'd go to Cambridge—where I subsequently studied for six months, in 1945. In Cambridge I was with my brother, who also studied art, as he had done in Leeds. After eight months in Cambridge, we went on to London. We were interested in sculpture mainly. As we had to do life drawing for a certain number of hours each week, we attended three or four different evening classes. But there was a problem with the heating; there were few possibilities to heat the classrooms. So we were on our way. One day, we went to a school—the Borough Polytechnic—to study life drawing, and the teacher there was David Bomberg. It was not that I sought him out; I didn't even know his name. My brother and I went into the class and began drawing,

and there was this man who was not like other teachers. I studied with him for about six to eight years.

Hans Ulrich Obrist — **Recently in London I talked to Sandy Nairne, who is doing a Wyndham Lewis exhibition ['Wyndham Lewis Portraits', National Portrait Gallery, London, 2008]. What was your relationship back then? Did you have access through Bomberg to the English modernists or their manifestos?**

Gustav Metzger — Yes, absolutely. David Bomberg was extremely talented, and even as a young man he was seen as an important artist. There's also the question of whether he had an influence on Wyndham Lewis. Wyndham Lewis was, I think, a bit older, and it's most likely that Wyndham Lewis learned from him. There was this situation when Wyndham Lewis started a movement that was called vorticism. He went to Bomberg and asked if he would join him, if he would sign a manifesto. But Bomberg turned it down radically. He had never been a vorticist; he was never formally associated with Wyndham Lewis and his group. Bomberg told us all about it, and he told us that [Henri] Gaudier-Brzeska, the young sculptor, once attacked him physically during a discussion. So Bomberg was a vital part in one of the most significant developments in the art of the twentieth century in Great Britain. That was important to me and all the other students. He was history. He was also a strong person—physically strong, too, very striking, and very aware of what has quality. We all learned a great deal. By 'we' I also mean Frank Auerbach and Leon Kossoff, amongst others. They worked in the same class with my brother and me for years.

Hans Ulrich Obrist — It's interesting that Kossoff and Auerbach painted in a similar spirit to Bomberg. After your years with Bomberg you soon transcended painting—you destroyed painting, if you like, as part of auto-destructive art. But something that has never disappeared since the time with Bomberg is your practice of drawing. One day, some years ago at a conference in England on the future of art schools, you called for the return of drawing to art schools. You've also worked on a large block of drawings in recent years—dozens of drawings that haven't been exhibited yet, but which you showed me recently in London.

Gustav Metzger — People have been drawing for many thousands of years. In the Renaissance, artists and art connoisseurs said that drawing was the basis of art. This is the case not only in the Renaissance, but in other periods as well. I also believe that drawing is the starting point of an artwork. Paintings begin mostly—not always, but mostly—with a preliminary drawing. I'm lucky to have a studio. One day I realised that I had to start drawing in this studio, because in one room—the upper room—the light is particularly complex and fascinating. That's where these drawings you've seen emerged. In the future, I hope to continue drawing, and I want these drawings to lead to paintings.

Hans Ulrich Obrist — Another thing I wanted to ask you pertains to the connection between your new lectures and the manifesto-like campaigns you've developed in recent months. You've referred to it as 'returning to agitation', and you've told me several times now about the importance in this context of the 'Breaking the Rules' exhibition at the British Library. The show was about the printed aspect of the European avant-gardes

from 1900 to 1937. Could you tell us about the exhibition and explain why it was so important to you at the moment you returned to agitation?

Gustav Metzger — This is a central question we're both very concerned about. The exhibition was unbelievable. You arrived and went downstairs, where it was necessarily relatively dark to protect the exhibits. Some of them were very fragile and extremely precious and unique documents. So you went down into a cave, a wonderland, where you almost had to feel your way with your hands to get through. Everywhere, to your left and right, and in front of you, there were cabinets with documents—I think more than 400 documents in total. In addition, there were films and reproductions of old films from the twenties and thirties. It must have been the work of years for the people who developed the exhibition, especially the head of this department. And what you saw was agitation. These documents agitate; they are offensive; they deal with energy and struggle—with ideology. I think this is the word that's essentially lacking in the art world today. I believe that, without ideology, without a conglomeration of ideas, of concepts, the art of the last 100 years could not have happened. But where is ideology nowadays? Where do you find artists publishing manifestos that might get into the British Library? I'm searching, and I can hardly find them. This conglomeration of ideas in this room, in this exhibition, was extremely affecting and stimulating. I'm sure other visitors felt the same way.

Hans Ulrich Obrist — This leads us to our next Marathon, which will take place in October in Frank Gehry's pavilion at the Serpentine. After the Interview Marathon and the Experiment Marathon, there will be a Manifesto Marathon, where fifty artists and architects will present their manifestos for the twenty-first century. In the sixties and seventies, you frequently wrote manifesto-like texts, which are compiled in a book.[25] One of my first encounters with your work was the catalogue *Art into Society* for the exhibition of political German art in 1974.[26] Have you developed manifestos during this new phase of agitation?

Gustav Metzger — Manifestos, no. Not until now, but it's under discussion. Regarding agitation, though… I could touch upon an aspect of the present situation: the feminisation of art, which is on its way—or, rather, on its way in the sense that curatorial courses are now attended by women in particular. As far as I know, the first one, at least in England, took place at the Royal College of Art. It was founded by Theresa Gleadowe, who is the wife of Nicholas Serota. That was a great idea, this course for curators. I regularly visit the exhibition every year; it's hard to find a man in a group of twelve graduates. I don't know about the other courses, but I can imagine that mostly women attend these curatorial courses. Women are breaking through the so-called glass ceiling. I see this as an issue because of the necessity for art to become more and more radical, more and more aggressive. We don't have the opportunity to discuss the matter here, but I'm sure this discussion will take off. Women in our society, historically

(25) Gustav Metzger, *Manifeste Schriften Konzepte* (Munich: Verlag Silke Schreiber, 1997).
(26) Christos Joachimides, Norman Rosenthal, *Art into Society – Society into Art. Seven German Artists* (London: Institute of Contemporary Arts, 1974).

speaking, have been brought up not to be as aggressive as men, not to fight like men. But, as I've said, we must be aggressive nowadays: we must fight, as artists, as individuals, and in a social context. To survive, society has to fight against the self-destructive environment in which we live. We have to talk about this, and talk about it publicly. I don't want to attack women. The exhibitions I was lucky to be part of, that were about my work, were organised largely by women, our relationships were very good, and the cooperation was at the highest level. It's just something I want to throw into the discussion today.

Hans Ulrich Obrist — **I have one last question for you. You've always answered my question about your unrealised projects by intimating that all auto-destructive art was an unrealised project—in other words, that many of the monuments of auto-destructive art remain unbuilt. However, some of these projects have been realised in recent years. I'm thinking of Sharjah and also of the skulptur projekte in Münster. How would you answer my question about unrealised projects today?**

Gustav Metzger — Sharjah was one of my greatest experiences, although I was not there in person. It's important to say that this project only came about thanks to a critic—an author by the name of Eva Scharrer. She's a young German woman living in Basel, who writes reviews for *Artforum* and other magazines. Suddenly, overnight, she was invited to be one of the curators of the Sharjah Biennale. She accepted and immediately proposed that we do the piece with the 120 cars. She fought for months to get it realised. In the end, there were 100 cars that fed their exhaust into a big tent-like structure. There's a very exciting video of the work, taken from a helicopter hovering above this large site with the cars. So that work has been realised. In Münster, these stones were placed day by day in different locations; it was done perfectly, again in cooperation with Kasper König and two curators. The curator that was especially involved with this work was Dr. Carina Plath. She also made an exhibition of unrealised models. So some things happen, and I hope to carry out more and more.

Hans Ulrich Obrist — **One last question—the Berlin question. What does Berlin need, Gustav?**

Gustav Metzger — *Me.*

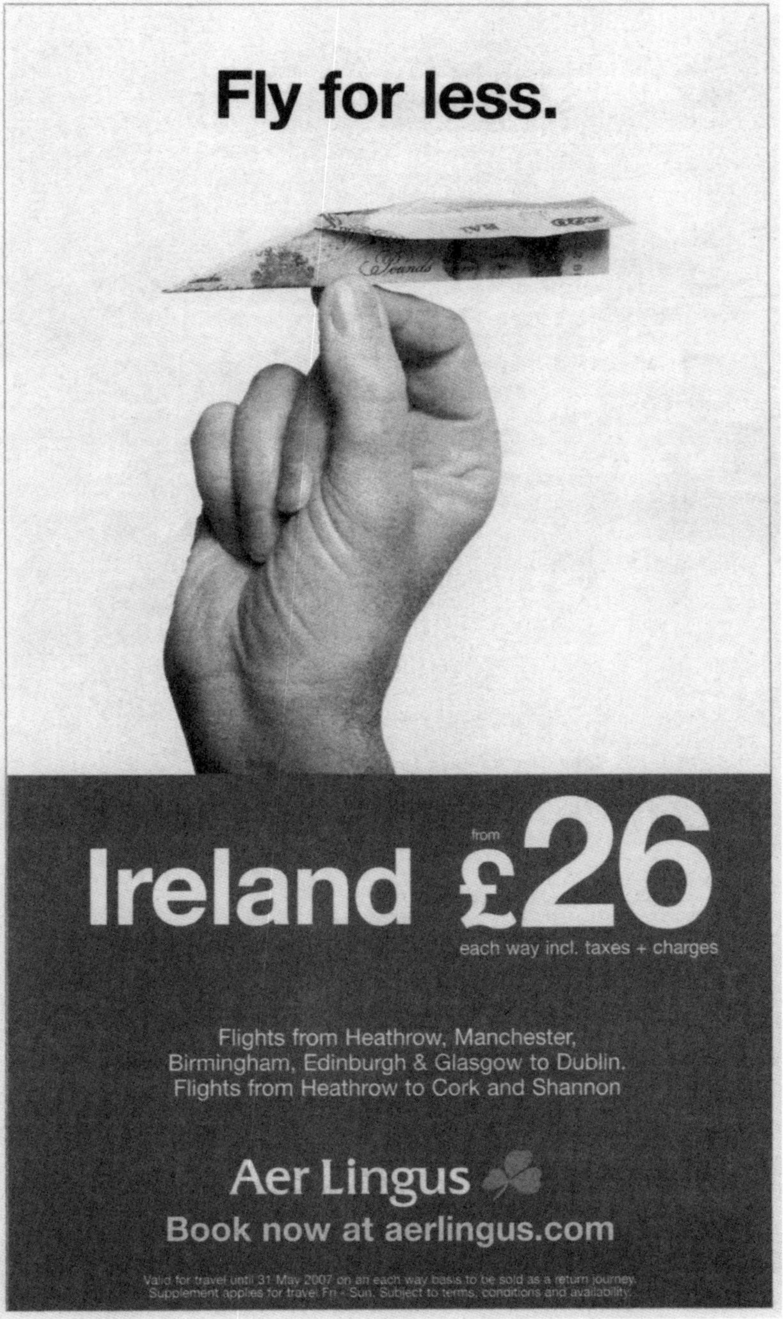
Fly for less.
Ireland from £26
each way incl. taxes + charges
Flights from Heathrow, Manchester,
Birmingham, Edinburgh & Glasgow to Dublin.
Flights from Heathrow to Cork and Shannon
Aer Lingus
Book now at aerlingus.com
Valid for travel until 31 May 2007 on an each way basis to be sold as a return journey.
Supplement applies for travel Fri - Sun. Subject to terms, conditions and availability.

Gustav Metzger

Born in Nuremberg, Germany in 1926. Artist and political activist. As a son of Polish-Jewish parents, he came to Great Britain as a refugee under the auspices of the Refugee Children's Movement. He became stateless in 1948. Metzger developed the concept of auto-destructive art and is known today as one of its leading exponents. He is also recognised for his protests in the political and artistic realms, and spearheaded an art strike movement in the 1970s. He published the first auto-destructive art manifesto in 1959. He was a founder member of the Committee of 100 in 1960. He participated in the first Fluxus event in Britain at the ICA in 1962, and initiated the Destruction in Art Symposium together with John Sharkey and others in 1966. Metzger has continued to create challenging works of art around the world. He currently lives and works in London.

Hans Ulrich Obrist

Born in Zürich in 1968. Since 2006 he has served as Co-director of Exhibitions & Programmes and Director of International Projects at the Serpentine Gallery in London, where he currently lives and works. From 1991 to the present, he has curated 150 exhibitions in various fields of contemporary art. In addition to these projects, he is the editor of a series of artist books published by Verlag der Buchhandlung Walther König.

Thanks to
(in alphabetical order)

Herbert Abrell
Marina Abramović
Michael Amzalag &
Mathias Augustyniak
Markus T. Andresson
John Armleder
Daniel Birnbaum
Stefano Boeri
Erica Bolton
Francesco Bonami
Laurence Bossé
Nicolas Bourriaud
Thomas Boutoux
David Bussell
Mathieu Copeland
Olafur Eliasson
Maria Finders
Hu Fang
Matthew Gaskins
Joachim Geil
Douglas Gordon
Jens Hoffmann
Anne Judong
Dorothée Kirch
Franz König
Kasper König
Walther König
Rem Koolhaas
Akiko Miyake
Stéphanie Moisdon
Isabela Mora
Yoko Ono
Suzanne Pagé
Beatrice Parent
Julia Peyton-Jones
Maria Platte
Alex Poots
Christian Posthofen
Jane Quinn
Emma Ridgway
Norman Rosenthal
Beatrix Rut
Angeline Scherf
Francesca Spickernell
Jean-François Taddei
Sally Tallant
Mizusawa Tsutomu
Lorraine Two
Barbara Vanderlinden
Eva Weinmayr
Jonathan Wingfield
Cerith Wyn Evans
Hafthór Yngvason

The Conversation Series.
Hans Ulrich Obrist

Already published:

The Conversation Series 1.
Robert Crumb.
Hans Ulrich Obrist.
ISBN: 978-3-88375-948-7
€ 9.80 / CHF 18.50

The Conversation Series 2.
John Chamberlain.
Hans Ulrich Obrist.
ISBN: 978-3-88375-922-7
€ 12.80 / CHF 24.–

The Conversation Series 3.
Konrad Klapheck.
Hans Ulrich Obrist.
Hans-Peter Feldmann.
ISBN: 978-3-86560-035-6
€ 12.80 / CHF 24.–

The Conversation Series 4.
Rem Koolhaas.
Hans Ulrich Obrist.
ISBN: 978-3-86560-077-6
€ 9.80 / CHF 18.50

The Conversation Series 6.
Wolfgang Tillmans.
Hans Ulrich Obrist.
ISBN: 978-3-86560-133-9
€ 14.80 / CHF 27.50

The Conversation Series 7.
Yona Friedman.
Hans Ulrich Obrist.
ISBN: 978-3-86560-171-1
€ 14.80 / CHF 27.50

The Conversation Series 8.
Zaha Hadid.
Hans Ulrich Obrist.
ISBN: 978-3-86560-078-3
€ 14.80 / CHF 27.50

The Conversation Series 9.
Gilbert & George.
Hans Ulrich Obrist.
ISBN: 978-3-86560-217-6
€ 16.80 / CHF 31.–

The Conversation Series 10.
Thomas Demand.
Hans Ulrich Obrist.
ISBN: 978-3-86560-204-6
€ 16.80 / CHF 31.–

The Conversation Series 11.
Nancy Spero.
Hans Ulrich Obrist.
ISBN: 978-3-86560-322-7
€ 14.80 / CHF 27.50

The Conversation Series 12.
Dominique Gonzalez-Foerster.
Hans Ulrich Obrist.
ISBN: 978-3-86560-334-0
€ 16.80 / CHF 31.–

The Conversation Series 13.
Olafur Eliasson.
Hans Ulrich Obrist.
ISBN: 978-3-86560-335-7
€ 16.80 / CHF 31.–

The Conversation Series 14.
Philippe Parreno.
Hans Ulrich Obrist.
ISBN: 978-3-86560-340-1
€ 16.80 / CHF 31.–

The Conversation Series 15.
Enzo Mari.
Hans Ulrich Obrist.
ISBN: 978-3-86560-401-9
€ 12.80/ CHF 24.–